Sorcha,

Thank you for all of your help during the Belfast Book Festival.

Please accept this small gift on behalf of everyone here at the centre.

Keith

LUNG SOUP

LUNG SOUP

ANDREW ELLIOTT

BLACKSTAFF
PRESS

BELFAST

First published in 2009 by
Blackstaff Press
4c Heron Wharf, Sydenham Business Park
Belfast BT3 9LE
with the assistance of
The Arts Council of Northern Ireland

© Andrew Elliott, 2009

Andrew Elliott has asserted his right under
the Copyright, Designs and Patents Act 1988
to be identified as the author of this work.

Typeset by IMD Typesetting and Design, Kent
Printed in England by Cromwell Press Group

A CIP catalogue for this book is available
from the British Library

ISBN 978-0-85640-838-0
www.blackstaffpress.com

Acknowledgements are due to the editors of the following publications in which some of the poems in this collection first appeared:

Aesthetica, Ambit, Magma, New Writing Scotland 24,
Poetry Ireland Review, Poetry Review, The Cortland Review,
The London Magazine, Times Literary Supplement,
The Yellow Nib.

In a very big city, a very big man
is pursuing me like he means me great harm.
How infrequently he gives me so much as pause for thought
is a testament to how (his fingers all but round my throat) I wear him like a cloak.

Contents

LUNG SOUP

ROBOT ATTACKS TWO WOMEN

BACK STORY

LUNG SOUP

Sometimes I Think of You

It's a house that could have sprung from a mind like the mind
      this poem's from –
cast in the shape of its shadows by a moon with not one but two men
      on it,
the moon only being there to reflect on what two boys could be playing
      at on a kilim –
while out in the woods that surround it wind swings in the trees like
      a big band.

*

Though no one knows it yet, tonight is the night that aliens land, their
      ship falling short
of garden, gazebo, and so prompting both boys to cover their eyes, sit up
      and turn out
... to be girls? Girls after all I see now, though those crew cuts they had
      me confused,
while crackling in static like a campfire, Judy Garland sings
      'Over the Rainbow'.

*

Time passes (time does ...) and the girls, they continue to wrastle like
      their mothers
might have sat there and knitted a black scarf or a white scarf or even,
      if minded, a cardigan
while aliens, en masse, to the glass of the French doors cling like spawn,
      dilating at first
then contracting when a torch at the top of the stairs is followed by the
      flash of a gun ...

*

The wheeling torch! The gun like the brush of an expressionist painter!
To have travelled for a thousand light years and happened by chance
    upon *murder* ...
From deeper still in the swampish night each gust brings word that
    death's black train
it's a-comin!, sung to the shunting Negro beat of a chain gang's shuffling
    home-bound feet.

*

But the girls, they're quick, they're nimble and they flee, clean-heeled,
    clean-hipped
like nymphs, picking hairs from their tongues as they run back to the
    pond in the woods
where the heads of weeping willows shake like so many air guitarists to
    come, bent
to their own reflections, to their own interminable sorrows. Not a baldy
    among them!

*

It's the eye of the storm. Let's catch our breath. It's a long poem. I'd
    forgive you for yawning.
Still, it's nice to have the chance to recall how it came to me walking
    through Somers Town
and how – *No pen!* – I panicked, until there on the pavement in front of
    me was one of
those little red biros you can pick up all too easily in bookies'. Countless
    drafts later, I shriek ...

*

Girls! Girls! Were you born in a field? For having been of one green
    gelatinous pulse,
a thousand polystomic globs – come in good faith just to be there for
    Elvis – yodel, *Aieee!*
as the French doors flap and so big are their brains that it weakens them,
    their suckers no match for the gale
now rising like an orchestra from out of its pit, that bit where it sounds
    all too serial.

*

The glass vibrates as the last one succumbs – a little muted *phuck* and it's
  gone – leaving
nothing but their pearlacious lip-stains. And so no eyes are fixed upon a
  pair of legs so hairy
they could be those of the first Mrs Rochester, her stilettos illuminated by
  the torch
as it swings then loops the loop and stops bolt-upright like a mic at the
  chin of a crooner.

*

Yet the light that torch sheds, it is haunting and the storm goes wild –
  fortissimo! –
blowing aliens through the woods where they splatter – upon bole, upon
  bark – and evaporate.
But wait! A lucky one lands in a treehouse where two boys – I mean girls
  in kimonos –
find it like a Storyville greenhorn (*What's that racket?*) in the basket they
  keep for their dirty things ...

*

It mighta been politer if you'd ... sorta knocked, says the black girl peering
  down at him,
*But then again, you're kinda cute, you little guest from Outer Space ... Ah,
  quit squirmin' willya!*
The alien appears to be trying to speak, and a pink liquid gurgles from its
  primary orifice.
Aw! Let's adopt him ... says the white girl, transfixed, a lullaby taking
  shape on her lips.

*

But quick! Back to the house where the kilim has been kicked clean out
  of the way and from a door
in the floor, lying open, the torch beam twitches upwards like a soul in its
  search for salvation
until from deep in that cellar or souterrain there comes what we must all
  have been dreading.
It's as if the storm has gone out with a *BANG!* and the wireless can be
  heard playing Cage's 4'33".

*

Suffice here to say it all ends with two boys – two *girls*, goddamnit!
What's wrong with me? –
two girls cycling sunward like swans and who sing as they cycle
something poignant
like 'Out There in the Night' by The Only Ones, in their baskets two
litters of little ones
whose eyes have been thrown over their shoulders like ears for their cue
to join in on the choruses.

Breathless

Amy flings open the window and takes in two big lungfuls of *Berlinerluft*.
She hasn't been in Berlin so much as a day but already she can smell
    revolution
like she used to smell bacon in Boston, exciting, forbidden, beginning
    to burn,
blackening the edges of everything, buildings, windows, faces, eyes,
    the sun

and such ideas as she has hitherto held to be true – not bad ideas
    but ideas
which Sabrina would scoff at if she weren't at that moment preoccupied
in a room across the street from Amy's, sitting at her desk, writing
    a poem
the last line of which I intend to translate and use as the last line of
    this poem.

How two such ladies got to meet – despite the iron tram tracks
    between them –
is a story I had hoped I could tell here and thus pre-empt my readers
    with rifles
from adopting positions on rooftops, in doorways, even astride
    equestrian monuments,
and preparing to take the gratuitous pot shots that will have me
    running for cover

down streets already being criss-crossed by people holding on to their
    hats, hats
after all being important, though I don't have one myself, so I pop into
    a good haberdasher I know
where the nice young man is happy to help and one leaves feeling quite
    the dandy,
only to be brought up short by one's readers beneath their banners,
    browed and fisted.

Friends! Comrades! I begin. I could as easily just stood there and asked
    myself, ' ... ?'
like a man who's been painted into a corner may stare at the brush in
    his own hand.
Instead, I juke back in. My young man has held out his hand and
    I take it
and together we run, my young man and I, until, behind a door marked
    PRIVATE,

where we have stopped to catch our breaths, he scribbles on the back
    of my hat's receipt,
which – now he tells me! – I'd forgotten, the address of a teahouse
    he knows ...
When I get back to Amy's room a bullet meant for me has hit her
    dressing-table mirror
and the sun from between two buildings burns like a spider at the centre
    of its web.

These Lines

Try, please, to imagine this line like a red flag unfurling
and underneath it, black, a line of people marching
through snow so deep, so white this line would be invisible
it not for the line, the last, its task to hold up everything.

Der Wirbelwind

One sometimes finds oneself walking
through the square at the heart of a city,
on one's own amongst thousands of people
when *der Wirbelwind* descends out of nowhere

and without so much as a *May I?* whips
the hat from every man's head – homburgs, bowlers,
the odd tricorne, caps like steam being let off –
until the sky has been filled with a Brownian melee.

To some it is a cause of panic, to others a source
of hilarity, but one way or another we will all have
lost our heads to a carnival of emotion so familiar
to such women as promenade at that hour in the square

and whose hats are tied to their heads just as firmly
as their heads are screwed on to their shoulders.
In the midst of our mayhem they hold on to their hats
and roll their eyes to heaven like so many Joans of Arc.

When *der Wirbelwind* resolves, revolving, to go elsewhere,
drops all our hats back on to our heads and departs
the square like nothing had happened, it will come
as a great relief to many, to others as a terrible let-down.

The latter will spend what's left of the day drinking alone
in the kind of cellar where women, backlit by the lights
of the bar, sit prettily smoking on stools and watching over them,
while the former will burn the midnight oil, convulsed by

draughts, however small, redoubling their efforts to hold on
to what's dear to them. In the morning the square will be
much as it was, the women will stroll that little bit taller
and the men will pass the time of day, the sun turning slowly

their shadows like cogs, turned in their turn by the handle
of a grinder until one man, a small man, otherwise unremarkable –
having called in sick the previous day and spent it by the lake
with his lover – comes whistling the tune that is in his heart,

sunbeams bouncing off his bald spot, and becomes aware
as he crosses the square that everyone's eyes are upon him ...
The whistling wilts on his lips and he stops, turns through
three hundred and sixty degrees, says *What?* and gets no answer.

Tresses

Sabrina is reading *Die Freundin* in the lobby of the Adlon Hotel
when, like an actress unsure where her next fan will come from
falls back on America like a suit of armour to deflect the glare
from the flat of her chest, not to mention how unlikely to bear

children her hips are, and makes a commotion of her own height
and hair, so red it renders Berlin grey ... a mind less cute than
Sabrina's might as easily have conjectured *Transvestite?* and put –
though I say so myself – their finger on a small point of truth,

though when I say small I mean so small that I could – even now –
let it pass and allow us to progress in so seamless a manner
that even those close combers who like nothing better than to take
a text slowly, tress by tress, might find themselves no more prepared

for the sudden appearance in stanza six of the face of none other ... But no,
now I'm late, I must hurry... Sabrina, having rolled up *Die Freundin*
and hidden it like a truncheon in her satchel – which contains so little
in the line of hard cash, that to pay for her coffee? she has no intention! –

then set off, like a torpedo, across the lobby, avoiding on her way,
like a *Who's Who* of Weimar, such faces as press into penumbra
those men like men no girl need know unless her straits are really dire
yet from whose midst (like the split in a curtain being searched for

and found) appears a young woman – a little bit flushed – who composes
herself on the Adlon's reception, smiles at Sabrina, fast approaching,
and says, *Ah, Ms de Wolfe, good timing! Let me now introduce you
to the love of your life, Ms Glinkelstein. Ms Glinkelstein – Ms de Wolfe.*

A Pair of Paintings

Sabrina

Of the many types of cigarette a woman can buy quite openly
on the streets of Berlin, Sabrina tends to opt for the Moslem
because of its red fez trademark, or the Turkish taste of a Camel
like the Camel Sonja is smoking in the painting by Christian Schad.

Amy

Sometimes Amy feels that she's walking around in a hat
like the lady on the left is wearing in Kirchner's Potzdamer Platz:
were she to take it off her hair would be all up in arms, as if the wind
were a stylist so maddened by the wind he no longer knows his own mind.

Caravan

I once gave a girl called Judith a bubblegum card of George Best –
of which, to be honest, I had dozens – in exchange for so tiny
a heart-shaped shell that the sea could as easily have forgotten
for how long it had been in its mouth, languishing in its own saliva,

or the taste of what it was had lived in it, before it spat it out
on the beach, where Judith had found it that morning, and which,
pink in the palm of her hand, beneath the gas mantle's bad light,
she told me was one in a million, took a deep breath – *Don't break it!* –

and afterwards gave me a little tin box full of cotton wool to keep it in.

What Ulster Means to Me

I sometimes like to think, when I'm driving through mid-Ulster
on weekday afternoons in June or early July,
of the wives men leave from nine to five to fend, as it were,
for themselves, bring up the children, keep clean the home,
pay the bills, do the shopping, prepare meat-heavy meals
garnished with suggestions of salad, yet who somehow manage
to find the time to have a little moment to themselves,
a duration that the faintest of breezes will fill with
bee-hum, birdsong, the rattle of a drum from a distant hill
until the sun on a passing car's roof stains the bedroom ceiling red.

Great Beauty

Amy is not a great beauty – lipless, hipless, I could go on –
but her red hair is to the wind what the word wind
is to the mind of a woman like Sabrina who can remember
the red flags flying from the guns of the ships in Kiel harbour

and who would later take the train to Berlin in time to hear
proclaimed too late – from a balcony of the Kaiser's castle,
backlit by crystal chandeliers – in words that were carried away
by an east wind bringing to the twilight snow like a message

indecipherable to all but the few, that Sabrina should pass herself
off as a boy and find herself rising on a steep learning curve
at whose pinnacle her heart was to glow like a star and then
come falling back to earth like a charcoal sketch by Käthe Kollwitz

of a woman in whose eye, had you been there ... standing behind her ...
waiting for a tram ... watching her watching ... over her shoulder ...
you'd have noted like an ember ... flaring in the wind ... Berlin,
like a strongman, having brought them so close, preparing

to part them like a chest expander ... when suddenly the wind
blows Amy over (as gusts can do to all such tall, untethered things)
and Sabrina, looking neither left nor right, shouts, *I'm a doctor! –
L'me through*! It fools no one but people are people, what can they do?

Hail a cab! shouts Sabrina, cradling Amy, who's a little concussed,
in her lap. A cab in its own good time pulls up and Sabrina asks,
Where do you live? Amy, oddly, can't remember so Sabrina
says, *I'll take you to my place* ... She shouts an address in Wedding

and the driver, like a Doberman pinscher, would have sniffed at it
over his shoulder if Sabrina hadn't snapped, *And where the hell
are you from driver, Dalldorf?* Had I been that driver I'd have driven
like the wind drives all before it with an eye on the rearview mirror.

AD 9

Had I been a man, the Hugh Hefner of his day, whose coffers
had risen like fountains just as round him the fortunes of Rome rose,
I'd have built a fine villa in the hills and kept there an odd number
of slave girls, testament to my reach and my axiom: *Every tree
that we cut down leaves ignorance one less shadow to hide in.*

At the end of each month I'd have marked up my profits and slipped
out of Rome for my villa, where a wonderful meal would await me,
after which I'd have loosened my toga and called all my girls to come
hither. *Bring candles!* I'd have shouted at the top of my voice
as the girls from my gardens and kitchen came, each shielding her

flame just under her chin like one would do the head of an infant,
and then made themselves comfortable on my floor, arranged to me
as I would have taught them the provinces to Rome were arranged ...
I would have begun with some innocuous chitchat, little things
I'd have picked up in The Forum, at which I might have raised a titter ...

Oh don't! I would have said then led them on – one thing leading, after all,
to another – so that soon out of the corner of one eye or the other
I would have caught a girl succumb to the trembling girl beside her
until every girl but one would have been trembling in the arms of
        another ...
It would have been as if my hand had passed palm-down across a map

and given me so great a pleasure that I'd have closed my eyes and seen
their breaths, a polished gong, being held for me to breathe upon,
Good night, my loves. Sleep tight! When every love but one had gone
I would have whispered to the dark that stood in wait, one candle strong,
Take courage, my child. Take courage ... held out my arms and howled.

The Beginning

It's a little modern kitchen like a kitchen by Schütte-Lihotzky.
Let into the wall there's a window, one foot by one foot
at head height, like a monochrome print called *Storm Clouds
with Zeppelin*. There's a pot on the stove and its lid's tinkling

in accompaniment to a gramophone playing jazz – *I'd love to say
I told you so but I can't cause I didn't so I won't* – while the couple,
at the improvised table, adopt expressions of such languid disdain
when the Volksempfaenger from the flat next door competes

by broadcasting *Die Meistersinger* ... With her face severely axed
by the edge of a cone of light, the ring of smoke she blows
from lips glossed red with whiskey wavers through the air and –
as if pretending to be tipsy – reforms itself into an ear which hovers,

like a question mark, expectantly, making it easy for a sweetness
to be slipped through the wall which her dinner guest has constructed –
a guest, it needs saying, who's a woman, a Yank and much older
than herself – from a lifetime of all theory and no praxis.

Still, she'll slip it, be assured ... but not yet ... Not, that is, before the plot
has got as twisted and bloodied as the knife in the pocket of that man
in trilby, trenchcoat, spats, who's been standing in the rain for hours
propping up the classic streetlamp, by the light of which he reads –

despite its turning into pulp – a copy of the Führer's *Mein Kampf* ...
Here, try it, says Sabrina. Amy takes it, laughs, holds it aloft. *My Torch
of Freedom!* she cries and will be lucky to live and have no regrets
when in a little room in Mount Sinai, *That can't've been us? Or can it?*

she'll sigh as the morphine surges one last time and the eyes
in the trees are beginning to blink, blinking back tears and going out ...
*Cycling so straight-backed? ... Steering one-handed? ... Stretching out our necks
for a ...* until the light has grown so bright and across it is written, *Ende.*

Love in a Frankfurt Kitchen

I built the prototype of a 1.9 by 3.4 metre kitchen and
I measured with a stopwatch how long it took to do
certain tasks. It has been saving women time for years.

MARGARETE SCHÜTTE-LIHOTZKY

Kitchens have come a long way and they'll probably go a lot further
but when in the future people look back this will be one they'll
    remember
and think of perhaps as a turning point, perfection's point of departure ...

The kettle contracting in the moonlight, the crumbs of comfort
    like boulders
to a mouse who ticks, plate to plate, having come not unlike an explorer
to where idle hands, going hand in hand, were led astray by pleasure.

Waiter

The window at which they sit depicts a sky going up in flames
like skies in the years to come will all inevitably do.
Tonight however it contains, moving from the left to the right,
a solitary Heinkel bomber. It is a prototype. It is on a test flight,

and its pilot, the bravest of the brave, flies more in hope than
expectation ... Having spent the main course, like a pair of pastors,
discussing, in earnest, Fear and Trembling, their brows by now
are almost touching and their lips become so witty with wine

that wearing expressions like a pair of clenched sphincters
their hysterical cycle has begun to spin down like a vortex that turns
into a feeling like dreaming and ends in the first unforgivable spurt ...
The smell of it smoulders and Sabrina, suddenly serious, quotes,

A rose by any other name would smell as sweet ... Hearing feet,
to stop herself from letting go, Amy waves for the waiter's attention
and Sabrina doodles in the condensation the heart through which –
even as it fades – he will watch them cross the rush hour street,

run for a tram and leave only the rank empurpled greens of a sky
going down flaked with flames, across which moves from right to left
that same now tried-and-trusted bomber, as he clears their table of plates
and wipes it, aware of their smell but unable to savour it, because

behind him stand, with their monocled eyes on his carefully kept hands,
two SS-Sturmbannführer, as if waiting for some reason, known only
to himself, to take him by the elbows and steer him, his metal tray
trembling for fear it will crash, through a door he won't believe existed.

Lung Soup

Sabrina has the kind of eyes which would put you in mind of her breasts
were you to have gazed, as Amy has gazed, into them over two bowls
of lung soup, in the kind of down-at-heel cafe where not to have
    two pfennigs
between you to rub would be to be thought none the worse of by
    the waiter,

a nice young man, doing his best to make ends meet, who'll note
    how clean
each bowl has been wiped as he carries them back to the kitchen to wash
and thinks of them running down late afternoon streets, afraid of him
brandishing in hot pursuit the kind of meat cleaver from which
    blood drips

until – being women of a certain age whose hearts have leapt like
    gallant boys
to their defence – they stop, look back and find themselves completely
    lost,
fog having fumed from every alley, bringing with it gangs of men who,
    sewer-brown,
blend into an army which stuffs itself down every throat as if, like TB,
    to attack

a pulmonary system weak for want of what? such air as patients take
    routinely –
their low-slung cure chairs parked aslant – from the balconies of sanitaria
whose cantilevered floors stack up, from densely wooded mountain slopes
on which the sun line's slow ascent is like a physician's hortative
    Chin up, chaps!

The waiter clears his throat discreetly. Eight hours later he'll hang up
    his apron,
deduct from his wages the cost of two soups, put on his coat, say
    goodnight,
and make his way to a part of town where the chimneys fly sulphuric flags
and where, given the lack of street lighting, it's a wonder he isn't mugged
    oftener.

What would you wager that on climbing up stairs, none steeper,
    he will open
his door and, breathing badly, feel for the switch like one would for
    a breast
and so shed light on the kind of room where it is only when one looks
    in the mirror
that one sees oneself over one shoulder waiting in bed with one's arms
    crossed?

Sabrina's Room

So great have been the pressures heaped upon it,
not only from the right but the left, that her room's
like a room by an expressionist painter whose paintings
are all painted with herself at the centre, her back

to the window in which the Reichstag's in flames
like a crystal crown splintering the sky, red and yellow
and in the meantime a ball – were a ball to be dropped –
would not so much roll as zig-zag, up and down the floor

all night like it can't find the spot where its thoughts
might be gathered, knowing like a head that there's a hole
in here somewhere and that it's got to get out before the pressure
gets too great and the building comes down to a big heap

of rubble. Only the bed approximates to being on the level
because books have been wedged between its legs and the floor –
books that will, in the months to come, fan the flames
like infectious hens and leave the shelves of the library bare

in the Institute of Sexual Research where Sabrina works as a secretary,
replying to enquiries from all sorts of people and giving to those
who turn up, like Amy, impromptu tours of the display cabinets.
My goodness, whispers Amy and Sabrina almost laughs, their faces

floating on the surface of the glass like the faces of two boys
on the kind of coast of which it could be said, *Wherever rock and water
meet no love gets lost* ... whose temples accidentally bump like shadows
on a pool in which they've caught their likeness *in flagrante delicto*.

A Walk in the Woods

At the painting by Emile Nolde, dated 1912 and entitled *Candle Dancers*
stands a man in a dark brown broadway who is protecting his own ass
with a homburg; in the presence of so much that is degenerate it is wise,
he is thinking, to be cautious, for there is truth, he believes, in the
    statement:

Wherever there is art, there's a risk. He checks to his left; there's a woman –
taller than himself; she's a redhead, with lips that look dipped in fresh
    blood;
she has about her that thing which screams *Jewess!*; when he checks
    to his right
there's a Negro who, bold as brass and blond, has a fox round her neck

and it winks at him! It is clear that both these women are obsessed,
    as if gazing
at themselves in a mirror in which he appears only as the darkness brought
    to life
by their candlelit dancing ... He snorts like a boar but gets nothing
    so he snorts
again louder than before ... Then he glares straight ahead at the painting,
    in a mood

like a wood in the middle of the night in which his mind wanders –
    Where's the exit? –
until it comes upon two elegant big tourers, leant together against the
    trunk of a tree,
their spokes humming something by Schoenberg. He just hugs his coat
    tighter – a flasher! –
and, looking right, looking left, he goes deeper, concentrating so hard on
    being silent

he's oblivious to the storm – *fortissimo!* – having placed him at the centre
    of a vortex
made of vapour-trails left by taper-tailed globules in each of which is what
    looks
like a homunculus, the latter splattering upon bole, upon bark and then
    sizzling
just long enough to evaporate ... He's so afraid of being heard, so afraid
    of being lost,

so afraid he'll break out in a sweat, that he cracks and whips out of
    his pocket
the *Hirschfänger* he carries just in case: *I will smite thee,* he bellows,
    I will smite thee,
as lunging he lashes *X-rated!*, thus expressing on behalf of us all what it's
    like to
have crept through that wood and happened upon two women candle
    dancing.

It is Amy – though thin she has a sinewy strength – who grabs hold
    of his wrist
and winds backwards, like she's winding back the arm of a clock ...
    The socket
dislocates and he squeals, the knife clatters to the floor and people,
    like trees
with the wind taken out of them, stand, very suddenly, still ...
    Good goin' stranger,

says Sabrina, who, assessing it all very coolly, takes Amy by the hand
    and shouts *Run!*

Poles

Soren: The Lost Years

There is no point my explaining how he got there
because a poem should be like life at its best – brief,
bold, cavalier, though doomed to contain inside itself
the kind of dungeonesque door on which *d-o-u-g-h-t*

has been scraped with a stick in blood and which
will always be guarded by goblins, bug-eyed in shades,
pugnaciously lipped, bandannaed, toting Uzis like gangsters,
who gesture you in, unmoved by your pleas, to the room

like a room that reminds me of a room by Mona Hatoum,
who lived in a room on Royal College Street in which I lived
for a decade, slightly later, with its bare 45W lightbulb hanging
to the right of a meathook whose shadow is the unanswerable quest-

ion from which you could find yourself dangling ... (this being –
before I go any further – the room in the poem ... not the room
on Royal College Street which was, I remember, a very nice room,
and, as part of a housing co-operative – of which for several

years I was Secretary and of which I'd have made a good Chair
except that none of the bastards ever asked me – at £14 per week
extremely reasonable) if it turns out you're so minded because,
let's face it, we're not talking a cell on death row here and goblins,

what's more, are not real. If they were they'd be happy to help,
blushing if you chucked them and whispered, *What really big boys
you must be* ... That or one night, while they were all sleeping,
you might have seen the door of your dungeon swing open

and despite your mind being completely blank, a pair of penguins
– *Where was I?* – making with their flippers to hurry up.

Soren's Head

No harm to it but, up to its eyebrows in snow, it's like an igloo
    throbbing hotly.
Inside it, like something gestating, there is the shadow of a man
    shadow-boxing,
inspired by the fight he's been watching on the holographic bay of
    his *Brainmail*
where, despite its being the kind of bout that might put one in
    mind of Schmeling v. Louis,

the girls wear gloves like cherry tomatoes that split on impact, flinging
    gobs of pugilismo
until the simile ends in such a big mushy mess that I am forced to
    confess, I nicked it ...
The ref steps in, he stops the fight and in the scene that ensues like
    a Weimar riot,
Sabrina 'The Wolf' de Wolfe, drenched in seeds, grabs the mic,
    That's it! I quit!

Oh! ploidy, ploidy, ploidy ... thinks Soren, logging off in disgust,
    When the fight game's
turned dishonest, what's a man got left to believe in? Who'd you nick it
    off anyway?
A guy called James Lasdun. I did change it slightly. *Course you did,*
    you schmuck,
but you reckoned you could get away with it, didn't you, you big fat
    homosexual,

softening them up with that quick one-two of 'igloo' and then 'gestating'?
    Expected
them all to be too punch-drunk to notice, did you? Please, before I vomit,
    how much
lower can a guy like you sink? Any damned sun in these parts and –
    you know what? –
I'd be walking off into it now. What the hell am I doing here anyway?
    It's fucking cold

and you've less than two stanzas to go; you gonna pull something out of this
    fire here?
He hunkers down and, like a trainer parrying punches with his palms ...
    Get on with it,
you schmuck, you make me sick ... feels himself become engrossed by the
    little flames
which duck and dodge with a mesmeric will which leaves him believing,
    She's a fighter,

She has it all. Those eyes of hers? The psycho-fight? It is over before it's even
    begun.
She's got the power, the speed, the jab, the hook. She was there all along,
    under my nose,
what a dope I was ... With his head in his hands he is a man in tears
    who cannot listen:
Will you stop beating yourself up about it, Soren. *Ding-Ding!*
    for Chrissake, *Ding-Ding!*

A Little One

When I was at school
there were girls so much bigger
than me. I miss them.

The Herero

The dentist's name is Doctor Fischer
and the girl he has in his dentist's chair
is a girl for whom he feels only repugnance,
representing as she does the infection of the race.

How dark the eyes are, no light seeps in there.
How lucky our little Kinder, whose eyes are blue
like windows so God can peep inside their minds
to see how all is bright and clean. No, we are not bunkers.

Her uncle's words come back to him – do they taunt? –
But Doctor Fischer, what am I to do? My brother
was my brother, should I ignore his dying wish?
These men of religion, don't you think, Doctor Fischer,

they fall with such ... with such amusing grace, their guilt
so like goodness ... And besides, I find her arousing,
I tell you this, perhaps I am not so unlike him after all ...
Doctor Fischer has never seen such perfect teeth,

white and strong and containing of decay not a trace.
With his stainless steel hammer he taps one a little harder,
no doubt, than he should do and it causes Sabrina
to wince. *Oh dear, oh dear, my little sweetness,*

he says and then he turns to his table of instruments.
Now please, he says, you must open very wide and you
must be a brave girl ... Backlit by Dresden's stone-cold sky
he nods to his pretty assistant whose colour rises like a flame.

A Brave Girl

In the poem you have started to read Sabrina will wear the glasses
and, apart from a rose tucked into a garter, so little else of note
that readers of a sensitive disposition may worry that by the time
this poem is over, she'll have gone and caught her death of cold

given the snow blowing by the window, which is twice her height
and on which she's just pulled back the curtain like the curtain
on a cabaret where the girls are hot and not averse to a spot of poetry
as might have been supplied by someone like Sabrina, whose talents

around now are beginning to unfold, dabbling in Dada and such shit
before finding her way to the novel, which begins with her leaping
from a dentist's chair, flying down stairs, through the arms of her uncle
and out onto the streets from where hearts can be stolen like stoves

to curl up at in little rooms rented by poets, typographers, an actress
called Gill, whose mind when left to itself felt neglected but whose
mother, she claimed each time wine touched her lips, was the duchess
of somewhere or other – a wonderful novel, full of freshness and colour

and dug, so she liked to say later, from out of that hole in her gum
which was to prove such a lucrative boon to the best dental surgeons
in Manhattan, whom she'd have steered clear of, not been for the pain,
opening her mouth like a lion about to bite the hand off whichever man

so much as flinched at the evil he found there like a grave in her mouth
and left her susceptible to breast cancer quacks such as Amy to her credit
would have none of. *Amy! You great big drink of ginger ale, look!*
she says. *It's* ... and stops, tips back her *Bubikopf* and shouts *Atch*OO!

Grunewald Weekend

Under tons and tons of darkness and moisture gradually increasing
Amy and Sabrina dream that they are walking through a forest
at twilight and, while such wind as rampages like a crowd through
the crowns is responsible for the falling of leaves through the branches,

all is quite still on the floor of the forest, where the trunk of each tree
has a message nailed to it, descriptions of cats, manifestos, recitals,
but mostly requests from the lonely for love with blurry photographs
or self-portraits attached, the older ones mouldy and already unreadable.

Yet so dark will it grow on the floor of the forest that only the leaves
like falling flames can shed any light on such black and white faces
as the dark will embolden to form a gang of their own, coming together
like a tightening stockade in which our two dreamers are suddenly trapped.

With her back to the wall of Sabrina's firm back Amy plucks a flame
from the air by its wick and holds it to the face of their laminated leader,
who is claiming to be lost, somewhere deep in these woods. When
        he offers
a reward but neglects to say how much, Amy wipes the rain like a tear

from his check. *Ow!* she squeals and lets what's left of her burnt leaf fall.
It is the rain which now puts out the flames, though not before Sabrina
has set light to a face and watched through her own black fingers
        in horror
like one would in a mirror one's own immolation. When sunbeams bounce

off buds like bells they will wake, face to face but on separate pillows,
the latter trimmed with lace like stamps, then rise, relieved, make themselves
a pot of coffee and take it, with honey, to the little back stoop where, sitting
still naked shoulder to shoulder, they will be by a pair of squirrels amused,

the helical pursuit of the one by the other unravelling in the branches
        of a dead tree.

The Great Depression

On the eve of her fortieth birthday, having sat for some time
at the window of the Stewarts' cafeteria on Sheridan Square,
Amy comes to the conclusion that she has grown unnecessarily old,
and her hands, palm-down on the table, are like a book she has

broken the back of. The story so far has left her cold,
and if it weren't for the snow – billions and billions of little flakes
like so many mathematical permutations being burnt off – she'd be in
two minds about finishing it. She thinks, *The world is full of little kisses,*

they happen here, they happen there, sometimes a kiss, it kinda misses,
keeps on goin' to who knows where ... She shivers as a gale of laughter
goes past her but she continues, *If I were such a little flake I'd look*
to land on a lip that's been bitten by the cold or there where a man has
        hit it ...

The laughing men are ordered out; for the last half hour they've ordered
nothing ... *Lie like a balm and be licked off* ... She nods to the waiter, a nice
young man. *Can I offer you a refill, madam?* There's a badge on his shirt;
it reads, Soren. Thank you, Soren, says Amy and then, *On good form*

tonight, our artist friends. He smiles but not unkindly as the men file past
in their WPA-paid-for coats, with their accents as thick as the scarves
they're winding round their throats. The last to leave pushes Soren aside.
The man is unsteady. She feels herself sweetened by the drink on
        his breath.

He says, *I saw you at my exhibition* ... Amy blushes and replies, *Yes, I was* ...
His friends are knocking on the glass to come on, pulling long faces
        as if to say,
Are you mad? Until he throws out his arms like that rebel by Goya, *And?*
Turning over her hands, Amy thinks, I'll give it one more chapter.

A Stencilling Machine

Had Amy been the kind of lady
for whom it had been nobler in the mind
to find herself climbing the stairs
of a stinking *Mietskaserne* in Wedding,

drawn ever onwards and upwards
by what sounded to her like the call to arms
of a Gestetner stencilling machine,
which she finally understands must be emanating

from behind that little red door in the attic,
to the keyhole of which she puts an eye
and sees backlit by the filthy skylight
an inky young woman who chomps her cigar

like the editor of a real newspaper might
were he to be the kind of man
who couldn't give a damn for his own well-being,
his beautiful home, his wife, his children ...

her neck could not have been placed on the block
with any greater sense of how vulnerable
such a lady's long neck can be, her eyes on a beetle
in the basket below, that swivels its head,

and pulls the longest face of all ... Before I, being the man
in charge, step in and, with all the powers
at my disposal, hold up that blade one neck hair
short of a neck from which all hope has drained,

thereby granting to Sabrina – past whom deadlines
have always flashed and meant so little –
the time to crash those gaol yard gates, shouting
Hold the front page! with her comrades, all guns blazing.

The World at War

Few things more upsetting, I guess, than being woken at three in
    the morning
by the famous German Tiger Tank appearing, gun first, through
    your wall,
it's commander, dusted with debris, momentarily a little dazed and
    confused,
extending to you and your lover – busy rubbing his tired eyes with his
    knuckles
like the captain of a submarine at his periscope – the old, not unfriendly,
    Sieg Heil!
then rolling on through, past the foot of your bed, with a hortative
    chop-chopping
of his forearm, leaving fumes which disperse only gradually to reveal
    what has long
been suspected, your neighbour in her bed with your wife who, instead
    of staying
over with her mother, has journeyed no further than next door from
    where – dust
settling like snow in the moonlight – she gives a little wave and grins
    sheepishly
as a soldier jogs through with a sub-machine gun, stops and retraces
    his steps, looking right,
looking left, till the truth dawns, whereupon he straightens his black
    Waffen-SS cap
and makes you all jiggle on your headboards, tickled pink as he shoots
    from the hip.

The Sailor

Let's try to think of Amy and Sabrina in bed as the bombers go over –
searchlights crossing in the sky like fingers while their legs are doing
anything but – and though it is, I concede, not a nice thought
in light of the fact that they're lit by the flames of the direct hit opposite,

like a depiction of hell as it might have been painted by an expressionist
set designer of the 1920s who'd have slipped out of town
on a train one night, got as far as Rotterdam and, having run out
    of marks,
in a room by the docks sucked off a sailor, who to his credit would
    have proved

as good as his word – though he could just as easily not have been,
    his word,
like the word of all the others who'd cut the line upon being swallowed –
when he took our young painter's head in his hands, lifted it up,
kissed both its eyes, licked its chin and said, *A nigguh's milk taste*
    sweetuh huh?

I would ask you, nonetheless, to entrust me with your thoughts like
    an heirloom
or a best china tea set and allow me to lead you up the stairs of
    that tenement
just as Amy had allowed herself to be led, though it could, for all
    she knew,
have been a garden path at the end of which would lie the gazebo
    of her ruin –

by Sabrina, who had, until that night, thought of her heart as her
    strongest muscle
and – the times being thuggish, not for the faint – more than capable
of packing punch after punch until love lay bleeding at her feet like
    a lesson
which she'd been taught at a tender age and to which she felt herself
    beholden

as she stood there searching for the key in her satchel like a knight
    might've
searched for the key to a castle and found it dangling from a branch
    in my brain,
the latter only now beginning to cool as the flames with which this
    poem began
leave me in mind of Winston Churchill and the opening bars of
    Beethoven's Fifth.

Birthday

Although it has been a year since an incendiary interrupted
their lovemaking – enflaming the bed and the pair of them
in it – only now have they mustered the will to slither, like gas,
from the rubble and take a walk round what remains of Berlin,

mingling – not so much with the people, of whom there are
relatively few – as with this mist which, rising, clings
and takes the sharp edges off everything. In the afternoon
they stop in what remains of a teahouse and Sabrina remembers,

Hey, it's your birthday! They pretend to order tea and *Sachertorte*,
then Sabrina strikes a match (or pretends to), plants it like a candle
in Amy's slice. *Quick!* she whispers, *Make a wish*. Amy wishes
for Sabrina and blows. Sabrina winks, *You got it!* then adds,

I like your horn-rim glasses, they make you look so brainy,
like you're peering through the Os of all the books that you've read
since the odd little thing you began as ... On the window which is not there
she doodles a heart that seems to say: *Though our bodies have gone*
    up in smoke,

combusted like bodies these days do, still, the flames they gave rise to
were something else! Then they walk for what remains of the evening,
stopping only to watch a young woman, her back coincidentally
to the wall on which her Daddy once daubed the yellow star,

still clearly there behind her head, and whose chin has come to rest
on the shoulder of the Russian raping her as if she is trying to count
how many men remain in the queue behind him but cannot
because it vanishes into the fog and continues all the way to Siberia.

Trümmerfrauen

Having more in common with the fog
than the rubble over which the fog creeps,
Amy and Sabrina continue to watch
until the girl passes out and the Russian,

catching her by her pigtails like horns
or the handles of a trophy he's won,
gives it to her once more like it might bring her
round, then allows her to slump, and to the next in line,

who wasn't feeling up for it anyway,
the opportunity to urinate on her cheek
presents itself as a blessed relief.
In the rest? Arousal? Pity? No excuse not to?

Amy and Sabrina push on through the fog
like in life they'd have pushed through
the boredom of life until two hands like two suns
reaching out from Siberia grab them by the backs of their collars.

For indulging in death like a luxury item
the summary sentence is *LIFE*!
and a commissar points them straight back to work
on what was once the *Mietskaserne* they died in,

already being crept over by so many
silent women, to each of whom the smell
has attached itself so sweetly like the smell
of a child being concealed by too much eau de cologne.

Writer

Who wouldn't have wanted to open his door in the winter of 1947
and find in his hall like death warmed up – though in neither case
warmed up fully – two women he had written off earlier.
Been me? I'd have played it as cool as that winter was playing it:

Back from the dead, are we? We'll see. Stood to one side and,
with an all but imperceptible nod of my head,
indicated that they should come in ... Cremated
in the loft of a Wedding *Mietskaserne*, buried under rubble, two years

blowing with the dust of Berlin ... I'd seen a pair of dolls looking prettier
to be honest, but that, I decided, was their problem. So, I said
You two gurls are back for more. I gotta hand it to ya, that takes ...
I was about to say *guts* but it suddenly occurred that they might not
    have any.

I pointed to the sofa. When I opened the stove to put on some more coal
the sight of the flames nearly blew them away and then when I asked
about their future their tongues were brittle
like leaves in the fall and capable of only one syllable: *Licht ... Licht ...*
    Licht ...

Another time, another place, two different dolls I'd've been only
    too happy
to have licked but clearly they were incorrigible. It was admirable,
I suppose, after all they'd been through. I was appreciative of their offer
but I told them no, maybe later ... What man, after all, ever likes
    to say never ...

I said, *What you gurls need is a complete make-over, not just new clothes
but brand new lives in a big new city. What you gurls need are ... visas.*
I thought I saw something come alive in their eyes, smiles cross their lips
like ships cross oceans ... They pulled on my heartstrings. I pulled on theirs.

The Bodies

It was during the famous *hongerwinter* – a time of dearth, enjoyed by all –
that I first felt my heart go a-boom-bang-a-boom-bang-a-bang in a dune
on the island of Texel, where I was hoping to take a new lease on life,
my old one having recently expired and gone down in a big blaze of legalese.

In a little wooden hut whose roof had long let in on ropes and old harpoons
and a shelf of lanterns rusting, I constructed a desk – as Dutchmen do –
from new bits of driftwood from long walks by the waves, then attached
a dead bulb to the ceiling with rope, alluding thereby to a poem I once wrote.

The North Sea boomed and banged that night as I churned out draft after
draft of my will until my head was a hell of the orphaned and ill, pleading
Pleasesirmesirpleasesirmesir like bullets intent upon my total destruction ...
I curled up on the floor underneath my new desk and tried to recall
    my dear

Marketa's voice, *Your dinner's in the dog, it's in the dog, woof woof,* that way
she had of calling me from deep down there at the bottom of our house
    which,
being so tall, one-window-thin (unlike myself, I'm fun-sized!), had me feeling
as I descended the stairs like *Self-portrait of a Man with Paintbrush and Luger,*

such would be my joy at love's anticipation – that laddish lock of hair she had,
with its refusal to be tucked away neatly behind the ear in which she suffered
from tinnitus, or the clippity-clop of her two clogged feet as she dashed –
onion-eyed – from the sink to the stove with the lungs I so loved in her red
    hands ...*Bang!* went the wind, *Boom!* went the guns until my brain had
    begun to inspiral,
*prompting me to think, Uh-oh, here comes Dr D if I am not mistaken and me
with my will uncompleted* ... Boom-bang-a-boom-bang-a-bang went my heart,
as I've mentioned already. Next thing I knew? I was living in suburban
    New Jersey

where the girls all – V for Victory! – had bodies like the lovely Jayne
    Mansfield's.

After Vermeer

It's a little modern kitchen like the kitchen you'd expect in the house
of a Dutch designer – so sleekly glazed yet out of focus
in light like electrified albumen ... Given the girl at the sink with
one leg missing is almost up to her oxters in a bug's eye of suds,

is she hiding something? Or, asks Detective Van der Jagt of Interpol,
whose journey this morning to Schiermonnikoog afforded him time
for a detour to a particularly interesting windmill, *Is it a red herring?*
Still, he thinks, what reason would she have to be washing, especially

under suds, a red herring? Better by far to have poached it in goat's milk
with a palmful of parsley and then added, at the last, like black magic,
a dash of some extraordinary soy sauce ... She is dressed in a nylon
white tunic, buttoned up the spine by small black dots, and her profile

is framed by the window, which is one foot by one foot at head height,
like a plasma screen showing over and over a scene from some sixties
sci-fi film, of a tiny pink spaceship descending, while her skin has that
same translucence in which pimples appear to float as in 3-D. In his rocking

chair Van der Jagt ponders: *Is it from the girl or from the sink that ...*
that leg is missing? While his passion is to be like Poirot, his hero, and not
be mucked with, as a detective in a poem, which he clearly is, he can only
be as sharp as he's allowed to be. So – rocking – he regards both girl and

sink, and thinks how, even dual-legged, she'd be pasty and, very likely,
an addict. He who – stale, bald, paunchy – prefers a girl as apple-cheeked
as the great Dutch stars of the seventies, who were limber in ways resembled
by Marketa – his wife, a childhood sweetheart – especially when it came

to the thigh department. How I weep when he thinks of them now ...
   Though
they were blamed by Marketa – *The thighs? The stars? for Christ's sake*
which? – in a note that he still carries – for the death of their love –
in his wallet. Yet his tune will change eventually when, at a little leaf-door

in Antwerp, a tinkling key on the cobbles like a fish out of water forces him
to concede to himself for the first time, *Though not necessarily human ...*

Spaceship Refuelling

Winter + Storm + Beach on the island of Schiermonnikoog = Greyness.
Or at least it would do were it not for the little fuzzy pulse of pinkness
which, about a mile out to sea, seems attached to the storm's umbilicus
by a thin blue vein of lightning, the latter lashing violently but continuous.

On the crest of a dune stands Van der Jagt contemplating what I've told him
is a spaceship, the storm having lent him an old Macintosh, a pair of welly
boots and an Ajax scarf, though the Macintosh he is finding quite useless,
it's the first one they made and has no hard disk. He chucks it away and

starts slapping himself – being as pink if not pinker than that spaceship –
when two big guys sprint by, neck and neck like wild geese, wearing nothing
but their gold-tinted goggles, though oiled up like eels for the shock of
    that sea,
its breakers rising like the workshop wing of the Bauhaus building in Dessau

(only, I suppose, a bit curvier ...). Smaller, balder, more paunchy, trying
    to dry
his old focals with his Ajax scarf, Van der Jagt remains calm and canny,
    having
noted that they run – as only two guys can run – hand in hand as they pass
those black man-high posts, and then plunge into the basement of a breaker.

Whereupon he thinks, *That spaceship out there, I wonder, are they friendly?*
Might not they smile on a man like me, so small and bald and pinkly perky,
when they themselves are Bondi-blue, their insides plain and all on show? Or
am I in the grip of their mind control? Oh! Look! Now it's rising ... There
    they go ...

What can a man do who has had thoughts like these but rip from his throat
the big knot of that scarf, and in the gloom, down the dune on his
    plump 'n' pink
legs, cut a dash like a cherub, only wingless, until at the edge of the sea like
    the base
of a cliff he must pitch himself in, hope for the best, himself against all
    that greyness.

Airwave

I have only seen a spaceship once. It was in 1954,
on the beach half a mile from Magilligan Point
when a greenness I'd been watching in the clouds
descended and, taking shape, I remember thinking at the time,

like that hat Mamie Eisenhower wore at her husband's inauguration
of the previous year, proceeded to float so close to the sea
that my view was obscured by the waves in that way
the sea has of appearing taller, like Alan Ladd, than it should do,

requiring me to stand on tippy-toe, jumping up and down
just to glimpse it, pulsing beams of green from its many concentric vents,
until, tilting a little to its left, it rose and – *This ain't the United States!* –
swirled round my head at such a helluva rate I landed on my butt

as it spun off and the only thing abducted – that day – was what I still
like to think of as my dignity, for what girl at that age would not at least
have been tempted by the thought of being swept off her bony big feet
by the tentacles of a greater intelligence ... even if it was only to wake naked,

fastened – limbs akimbo – to a stainless steel table with little grey men
performing upon her an extremely despicable experiment ... Oh, back then,
    in 1954,
could they not have seen on their ship's plasma screens a girl not just worthy
but willing, who'd've swapped on the spot her collection of shells, her
    parents,

five brothers and three sisters, not to mention that interest in contemporary
    millinery
which was destined so much later in her life (having picked herself up in '61
and found herself walking, all by herself, across the wet tarmac
of Shannon) to bear her fruit in the shape of

Keepin' a Lid On It: The American Hat, 1953–1999, for a spin in an
    expanding universe.

ROBOT ATTACKS
TWO WOMEN

Aliens

In October 1947 Mr and Mrs Suburban Vermont opened their door
and found on the stoop, backlit by as fiery a fall as there'd been,
a pair of men equally green at the gills, on the boards, by each
a quaint valise and no sign of the cab they came in. It hasn't hung around.

Allow us, please, say Mr and Mrs Suburban Vermont,
as they each take a case and lead the way up the stairs
to the spare room with its twin beds and between them the dormer
which is open like a painting called *Little Boy Eating Apple in an
    Apple Tree.*

The cases are laid, one to a bed; the little boy waves when he's waved to
and then Mr and Mrs Suburban Vermont, trying to remember
so many little things, propel themselves backwards by sheer
force of chatter and bow out of the door, which swings closed in
    their faces.

I am standing behind them when they regain their senses,
my arms around their bent old backs like Christ on his cross taking under
each wing the two crooked thieves who deserved all they got.
I am the apple tree boy's greaseball of a brother. They take my weight

as best they can and in return I lick their ears, delve into those
    glistering whorls
until there forms within my mind the question I'm compelled to ask:
How hairsome can one's folks' ears grow? When an apple pie pipes
at the kitchen window, our Mexican maid cuts me the slice into which
    she's put

her golden heart, so carefully wrapped in greaseproof paper. I kiss it,
she smiles and when, decades later, sitting by the fire of Thanksgiving
    together
– *Though wars may come and wars may go, you and me, we're different
    colours.* –
the ceiling creaks, it does not matter. We're here because we love
    each other.

North Korea

Amy and Sabrina have not yet met though they're living in a bungalow
    colony
where neighbour with neighbour is connected by wires and the lawns,
    having
stood for so long merely mud, are beginning to do what lawns have no
    real option
but to do, which is to proliferate the need for gardening expertise,
    something

which, when it comes in the shape of a man and his mower, can be
    a little creepy
so that the women of the colony stay home with their babies, the latter
    displayed
behind the Plexiglas screens of their Aircribs like pets or incubating
    anchormen,
television being still in its infancy and not something every bungalow
    can be relied

upon to possess, unlike, say, a cocktail cabinet so well stocked it has
    the appearance
of unreality and which in many instances results in telephones being
    left to ring
incessantly, for what, as Amy well knows, can a housewife do – once
    the cleaning's
done and she's been to the bedroom – but sit in the kitchen and indulge
    in a drink,

which is exactly what Amy is doing at a quarter past ten one July
    morning when,
across the fridge's man-high blur, a shadow drags her eyes in hope
    and there's a
knock on the door of her bungalow. When she opens up blinking,
    stunned by the
light, a clean-cut young man from the Airforce is apologising for having
    to inform her

of her husband's death, in August last, shot down during aerial combat,
    high in the sky
over North Korea, by a Soviet-built MiG-15 ... *If there is anything, you
    only have to ask ...*
Thank you, says Amy, *but in actual fact there is not.* She closes the door
    and thinks,
Husband? North Korea? Aerial combat? She tips her drink in the sink
    and continues,

*Amy, please, compose yourself. Big breath in ... Big breath out ... Now, there
    must be*
a photograph somewhere ... Only then, to her horror, the Aircrib, *empty!
    It's escaped!*
she screams. Boy? Girl? She can't remember. She searches frantically, then
    sits down
and flicks through a magazine, falls asleep, wakes again and thinks,
    Where was I?

Telephone rings. It be her baby? *Mommie! Mommie! Where am I?*
    She picks it up
and listens carefully. *Amy? ... Amy, this is your neighbour ... Miss Wolf ...
    You don't know me.*
*But that man called at your door just now ...? There is something I think you
    should know ...*
And as she listens, face to face with herself in the mirror, Amy thinks,
    Do my eyes look

*a little bloodshot? Skin a little white for my likin' ... That a moustache?
    I need to get out more.*

A Man of the People

Amy climbs on board the bus and the bus rejoins the evening traffic.
She is as ever intending to read but the sidewalk is no less compelling.
There, for example, at the door of a dive is a man so tall he's a head
above the competition, looking left, looking right, and despite the hair

he has remaining being as red, if not redder, than her own, he wears no hat.
Why is that? He lost it? He looks a little tight, it's true, but in the way
a poet might or a man of the people. It makes her think: *Men who're tall,*
their dicks proportional? If so, what would that man be like in the sack?

She pictures a dick like she thinks he might have. *Perhaps, next stop,*
I to run back and ask? (I'd have liked at this point to insert a disclaimer ...)
But the bus gives a jolt and had you been Sabrina, impatiently waiting
on the sidewalk to cross, you'd have felt it vibrate like an aluminum animal.

Backlit by the window of Macy's in bloom, with its new look, *The New Look*,
just in for that spring, do you see yourself fattened in its diesel-tanked flank
like a great weight keeps coming down, hard on your head? Or do you
    look up
and see her like a holographic saint – locked in by the glass, its grimy patina

yet framed inside a heart, lent her by some store interior – too quickly retract
and go back to her book and, when you look up again, become some Upper
West Side bitch who indicates her golden watch which, true to timeless Swiss
precision, reads to you like golden watches always do, It later than
    you think?

Then leaves you squinting at the sun's reflection in an office block window
pushed aside by a lady who is almost certainly Italian, even fatter than
    yourself,
mouth wide open. *No!* you cry, and the man behind you barfs routinely,
shrugs at your disgust and says, *I'm blocked. I'm blocked out of all proportion.*

Life Insurance

What'd be the weight, in tons, of New York? ... This feeling I'm feeling?
Does it need tranquillising? The war by now behind her, Amy's on a bus
headed home one day when a Negro takes the pew in front of her –
a tight-assed twin-set in tweed and wearing it with a blouse of cream silk.

Two tortoiseshell swans at the nape of her neck glitter breast to breast,
each street they cross as if the sinking sun's diminuendo were a period,
    pink,
in the gasoline green of a sky from which, later that night, so much snow
is going to fall there'll be neighbourhoods wake in the morning and think,

To hell with sellin' life insurance, I'm gonna take the day, spend it in bed,
they can me, see what I care. And then, half an hour later, *Ah Jeez, maybe*
I oughter ... Amy thinks, *This bus to brake, brake real hard? I kiss that girl,*
smack on the neck ... make it look in the jolt like I passed out ... Give a
    little bite ...

Taste what she tastes like ... I 'ginnin' to think like a vampire? As they pass
through the shadow of Metropolitan Life, like a blind man feeling
    for heads
he can count on, the black girl extracts from her handbag a compact,
What the hell's she starin' at? Screwy lookin' dork ... Suits the moustache
    though ...

When she snaps the compact shut like a trap, Amy feels her face has been
flash-fried, spat at, and it leaves her blinking hard at the sidewalk in fear
like a cine left running in a riot. *You got somethin' on your conscience ...*
ma'am? asks Sabrina to her face, having swivelled. *Do I know you?*
    asks Amy.

No, but you obviously want to ... C'mon, I know a cafe near here. You'll like it.
When Amy don't stir – *You deaf on top of all?* – Sabie snatches her big bag
from Macy's, allowing her thereby an excuse, no choice, it's up to her.
    Hey!
Stop thief! thinks Amy, leaping from her seat. *That's my heart you got in*
    there!

The Shadows

In a trenchcoat and so scarlet a scarf
that its reflection in department store windows
has her head twisting violently backwards
like a man has leapt out of the shadows
and is throttling her to death with her own scarf,

Amy has decided to walk twenty blocks –
rather than pay for the bus or the subway –
to the odd little cafe where Sabrina has promised
she'll be waiting at a table well away from the window
reading *Spicy Detective* or some such trash.

Amy walks a lot faster than most women would
and it's odd how it's mostly little men hold her up,
taking in Broadway like they've no homes to go to,
one of whom, to Amy's irritation, is ... me! I pull a long face,
bring down my shutters, hold up the palms of my hands

and say, *Fine, fine. Pretend I'm not here. You needn't
even thank me for existin'* ... Amy exclaims *Thank you?
I'm forty-four years old! I haven't so much as the dough
for a cab and you've got me walkin' twenty blocks
to meet some doll – so desperate have I got – who, given*

*that reference to Spicy Detective – which didn't go un-
noticed, I'll have you know – may turn out to have a razor
concealed in her soul.* Now this makes me mad.
Sabie has a gun in her satchel, it's true, but her heart?
Her heart's pure gold and I make that abundantly clear.

*Amy, my dear, you'll not only like her, you'll love her.
Now quit this nonsense. Dry that tear. No more o' these fears.
The only thing standin' in your shadow is me, you hear?*
I hail her a cab, I dab her eyes – *I'm a silly old moo. You forgive me? –*
and I wave her on her way like Sir Walter Ralegh, a gesture

that unfurls like her own scarlet scarf and ends at the door
of what would otherwise have been such a hard-to-find-cafe
where, sitting well away from the window, as promised,
so engrossed is Sabrina in her *Spicy Detective* that, when every other
second head swirls on its axis, she somehow neglects to notice.

Robot Attacks Two Women
A thrift store painting by Danny Hall

The painting depicts, as its title suggests, a robot attacking two women.
I have framed it in gold like it's valuable, and now on the nail from
    which I've
removed such a sweet little oil of a black rose, a white, I hang it above
    the bed
where, so moist is the night, my conscience must cover like a sheet their
    immodesty ...

Mindful that floorboards can be throaty like toads, I take one step to
    the door,
then another and feel the moonlight caress me, briefly, like butter,
    though butter,
I gotta say, that's gone a little rancid, must've been left out all day and
    then the day
it being so hot and all. You can picture it, a circle of yellow on its
    circular plate.

I only mention it to point up what a mess this could be. Someone to
    get killed?
That someone could be me! I'll tell you why. To see them there, sleeping
    like a pair
of sig runes, you'd never guess – or wouldya? – that beneath pretty
    pillows
they keep two little guns of a type gets made for ladies in a factory
    down in Arkansas,

by the kind of small, old-time concern any pap'd be proud to pass
    on to his son
until, that is, there comes a son, decides to sell, move to New York,
    become – *The hell!* – a painter?
The fucker! I blame his mother. And then what? I'll tell you what.
    He finds his
self standing in a cold-water flat, his hand on the knob of the door,
    looking back

at the painting with which I began all this – none of it, I emphasise,
  confessional,
for what makes a man ever want to confess, boohoo his heart out on a
  cop's fat chest?
The cop a little queer, maternal type of guy who'd run his tender fingers
  all through
your ginger hair while keeping to himself, *What a fright this guy'll look in
  Sing Sing's*

sizzling chair. No, lie till you're blue in the face. Makes sense, you might get
  lucky,
get to walk out the door of that courthouse, your head held high, and
  feel the sun
slap-bang on your mug like *You done it!* What a great feeling that must
  be. Like me
closing the door to the room where they'll wake beneath the painting I
  have left them.

                                    *

The painting depicts, as its title suggests, a robot attacking two women.
Of that, I believe, we're already convinced, although standing here now,
at the door looking back, I realise that I have hung it a little ... skew-whiff?
My conundrum is this: go back, put it straight, run the risk that they'll
  wake

or think *What the hell, it's already too late* ... My heart's in my mouth
  like a lump
of bubblegum and it's as if I've blown it when the floorboards croak
like not one toad but two, exchanging disgruntlements at their lot
  in life ... Butter's
still there on the plate where you pictured it – though you'll want
  to think better

of the roach that you've added like a beauty spot with two hairs growing
  out of it
and which could, all too easily, be cancerous. I to be you? I'd erase it.
  You wanna
know what I do? I'll tell you what I do. I avert my gaze like a man
  so fastidious
that were he to be tracked by one brown eye, one blue, there's a chance
  he would pass

like a ship in the night, carrying under his arm like a gift he has for them
    such a sweet
little oil of a black rose, a white, whose thorny stems twine in such a way
    as won't hurt
like the ruby-raw flesh of a boy once hurt when his pap took to him – for
    being less
like a boy than that pap would've liked – a belt of a type not uncommon
    in Arkansas ...

I tiptoe through books – Marcuse, Freud, Heidegger, Reich – until a
    mustard-yellow
platform pump nearly sends me like Superman, flying, fists first. It's the
    fright
of my life but I quickly recover, though I feel my back thrashed by a
    throb of blue light
as the hand I just happened to have free at that moment is reaching out
    to put right

the painting with which I began all this, none of it, I reiterate,
    confessional, for what
makes a man ever want to confess, boohoo his heart out on a cop's fat
    chest? The cop
a little queer, maternal type of guy who'd run his tender fingers all
    through your
ginger hair while asking of himself, *I wonder will his eyes fly forth
    like balls of fire?*

*

The painting depicts, as its title suggests, a robot attacking two women.
But what I thought then was this: *Some schmuck has gone and called
    the cops.*
He seen me from across the street? Them windows all look dark to me
*yet any one could frame a man whose own cold-water flat, I'd vouch,
    would look*

*a little sparse – perhaps a mattress on the floor, a gun hung up in its
    old holster,*
the telescope which he'll have trained to pick from out the black-backed night
*one lady's mane of ox-blood hair, one's bob of boyish brown. He think
    them red*
*in tooth and claw, a kind of communistic vamp, a type not easily found
    in Arkansas?*

Jeez! I think, *caught in the act, it's not how a mother likes to think of her son*
even if he's an artist and beyond all that ... I look up like a guy in search
    of salvation
and so see on the ceiling a circle so sallow that it must be the butter or the
    butter's
reflection, across which crawls like Sputnik 1, whose weeks of transmission
    had penetrated

my mind like a little metal gavel being brought down on metal, a
    cockroach such as
you have imagined. *All New York's finest run to fat and this block's got*
    an elevator ...
It's now my mind is moving fast and I take from the nail (large enough,
    since you ask)
the painting with which I began all this – none of it, need I tell you,
    confessional,

for what makes a man ever want to confess, boohoo his heart out on a
    cop's fat chest,
the cop a little queer, maternal type of guy who'd run his tender fingers all
    through
your ginger hair while whispering to you, *There-there* ..., though he, like
    you, will know
for sure there ain't no *there* where *Chair's* concerned – and replace it with
    their black rose,

their white. Avoiding the books, not to mention that pump, I take one
    step to the door ...
then another one ... until, where lesser men than I would pause to lift and
    steal a peek
beneath that sheet of moral fibre, with one swift sweep I pluck it off, am
    out the door
through which – taking stairs in twos and fives – I'll hear that fat cop burst
    and bawl, *FREE* ...

Abstract Expression

Hard not to envy Jackson Pollock his lack of a full head of hair.

A Rainy Night in Gotham ...

Panel 1

*How many tons of rain have fallen already tonight on a street
like a feng shui nightmare, where no two lines meet short of crooked?*
Raindrops tailed like molten glass by the lurid lights through which
    each slants
are pissing off a gang of rats who've holed up in a tipped-over trashcan.

Panel 2

There's a clocktower to the left; it reads midnight. Its bell has a crack
and says *Dang!* ... Being watched from beneath an old streetlight
by a man in a Fedora so rakish that his jawline is all we've to go on,
in a building so dark it looks creepy, there is one little window still pink.

Panel 3

From that man's hat brim raindrops drip and each contains that window,
at which now stands the kind of doll who doesn't give a damn for blinds
when she's undressing – drop by drop in quick succession – until, like tulips
at the wrists entwined, to the hasp of her black brassiere her fingertips attend.

Panel 4

Her shoulder roused like a cat being catty, she throws him a wink
and thinks, *He'll be so lucky,* as from a rifle barrel bursts an orange lily.
The blue-black towers behind the rain – falling still in whispering
    sheeeeeeee ...
ts! – background the bullet going so fast it has its own white-hot slipstream.

Panel 5

Let's interject a panel here and ink it in completely black, though at the
    bottom
leaving room for a little thought to bubble up – a gaseous green that's of
a type usually seen in labs where mad professors work – and inside which
the thought itself is so succinctly put: *DIE YOU VILTHY PEEZ OF TWASH!*

Panel 6

The bullet leaves a whizzing *hizzzzzzz* and that last crystal drop explodes.
Though guys with jawlines rarely think, *Gee, that was close*, thinks our
    guy now,
Perhaps tonight's my lucky night ... The bullet though has hit dead on
the dank old flank of that trashcan and the rats have scattered squealing
    Yikes!

Valentine's Night

Amy has opened a beer and sat down at the box for the fight –
Sugar Ray Robinson, Prince of the Ring, versus Jake LaMotta, Punk –
not so much for the fight itself as in the hope of seeing, ringside,
Sabrina, who's there to provide an account for the *Detroit Daily Star*.

Though the television couldn't be newer – an exuberance on the part
of Sabrina – the picture's poor and the flat is as cold as a refrigerator.
Amy has her coat on, a month-old hat from Macy's sale and a pair
of old fluffy wool mittens, *Like the colour of somethin' the cat'd cough up,*

as Sabrina has so tactfully put it. She can hear the Italians in the flat below
living it, punch by punch, on the radio until, by the end of the 8th,
to her own surprise she's thinking, *Sugar Ray? He's a class act but still,
LaMotta's doin' okay. I'd say it's even. It is* then she makes her big mistake.

She's had another beer in the meantime and now she thinks, *Yep,
I'll have a Scotch. It'll do me no harm. In fact – this sort of weather? –
it'll be positively medicinal. I ain't seen hide nor hair of Sabrina. Could love
have left me blind while truth is I'm bein' two-timed?* When the bell – *I ain't*

right yet! – tolls for the 9th she leaves it neat and takes a sip. *Goin' Sugar Ray's
way this round,* she thinks in the silence taking shape through the floorboards
so that, end of the 10th, refilling her glass, she overspills its brim and blubs,
I'm such a big romantic. All heart, that's me, that's my problem, just standin'
        there

*punch after punch, and her, the little bitch, too hot for her pants, in some little
hotel room in Chicago ... Hit 'im, LaMotta! Hit 'im!* By the time it's stopped
in the 13th round, Amy's slumped in her chair like it's caught her from
        falling,
lips wiped half across her cheek and, despite the television having gone on
        the blink

like a butterfly's wing in a matchbox twitching, Amy who never knows
when she's beaten, lies there thinking, *Boy, I needed that! We another bottle?*

Self-portrait as a Young and Inexperienced Poet

We were dining on crayfish, out by the bayou, the sun going down
on day so hot that the black hair bubbled from her oxters like oil.
Black gold, I thought as I talked and talked – touched by the sun? –
about poetry. *It bubbles up*, I said, so unable to repress the thought

of hair being bubbled from – where else? – that what I wanted to do
was knock a spoon on the floor and, with a self-deprecating *Oops* ...
leave her dining by herself except that, having finer feelings, I knew
that she would be embarrassed and so I just kept on talking about
    The Simile.

Best kept short, I said, *clipped if you like. What can happen otherwise is
    that the poem
ends up a mess, swamped and from its depths, like in them fifties sci-fi plots
that were always 'really' about something else, communism, the bomb ...
I was, after all, trying hard to impress. Like in a horror movie?* she asked.

That's correct, I said, but I'd an inkling I was wrong. I could feel the oil
seeping into my sneaks, and I was feeling somewhat desperate
when I went ahead and said, *At the simile I am, for the most part, adept.
I keep them discreet. – I see*, she said, her eyes on mine, *but please,
    continue,

elucidate. – Well*, I said, aware of the oil creeping over my lap, *these
    crayfish,
for example* ... She rolled her eyes, they were black like the oil, which
had reached the table top and could no longer be ignored, like two
    hands' slow
progress across the cotton cloth until – *Louisiana? This illicit?* – they
    blent ...

Which would have sufficed but there was no time to think, we were
    in it by now
right up to our necks, and I'd have cried out *Sheet!* had I not seen her
    wink,
dip her chin, demur and lick ... I took a little sip like I was swallowing
my panic. *But this could take us all night!* I cried and she replied,
    Uh-huh ....

My Aunties

Back when the US economy
was still rooting around in the dirt
for what all it would need to take hold
and become the great powerhouse we love today

my aunties were already growing old
in a little homestead in West Texas
where they lived and very rarely saw anybody
until, with the passing of the years,

if they hadn't had each other they'd've had no one.
For that (and the sky) they were grateful,
thanking the Lord each night in their prayers
for having had the foresight to bless them with each other.

And that ... that was about it really. No late-night chat shows
in those days, no B52s on their way to wherever.
When they died they died together in bed
for that winter'd been brutal and a great wave of snow

had rolled down from the north. After all what were they
but women? They had no rebuttal. When I found them –
two skulls, one pillow – their quilt a kerfuffle of rats,
I could tell straight away how a grave was required.

The sun beat down hard on the head of a fellow. I thought,
The deeper I dig, the purer the sky into which they'll be laid.
But when I brought them out tied in their quilt like swag,
it was indeed a great darkness had arisen. I was made.

Tinseltown

An oceanic *Boom!* shakes the shadow of blinds like bars far too flimsy
  to offer any protection to *The Birth of Venus* by Sandro Botticelli
reproduced on the wall above the seashell-shaped bed in which
Amy and Sabrina are only now waking up beneath a quilt of oyster-silk

and where, pleasant though it always is to wake and see a friendly face,
they groan as if repelled by the greenness of each other's gills, turn
their backs upon each other and, hooking their chins to the shell's gilt edge,
vomit into basins Amy had had the prescience to put in position before the
    limo

arrived the previous evening to deliver them to the RKO Pantages Theatre.
A win-win idea, she'd thought, *for a win-lose occasion*, about which now
she is able to remember almost nothing apart from the actual announcement
    itself –
And the nominations are ... And the winner is ... – and Sabrina's merciful
    failure to cry

followed by darkness, flashbulbs, faces like faces less life-like than they once
were and whose flesh begins to crawl when, across the flooded forest floor
of a night she'd thought could sink no lower, that German doll goes
and gets the hots for Sabrina. *Holy schmo!* thinks Amy, *I think I'll*
    punch her!

Sabie, dizzy, looks over her shoulder. Greenly bearded in vomit, she wipes
    it away
like a wise man might stroke it and quote from Confucius, *He say:*
Venus? The bars? I like it but look, what the punter wants here is nubility.
A girl, a gun, the gun goes off, second girl comes to the rescue, you get where
    it is

that I'm headed? Two middle-aged dolls like the dolls we are now? The punter
just ain't gonna buy it. Moreover he may find it obscene ... Amy, you okay?
Amy replies, *I suppose so ...* When they roll back together, a little less green,
they touch something hard in the bed in between them. Dildo? Sword?
    A figurine.

The Chair

In 1953, early in the morning of June 20,
Amy and Sabrina pack up a lot of stuff –
books mainly but also clothes, pots and pans;
old quilt Amy bought in a store on Bunker Hill

with a little loose change that she happened
to have in the pocket of her pants at the time;
blankets, sheets, a pair of pillows, a box of cans
containing food, a canvas tent and a bottle gas stove.

Then Sabrina locks the door and kisses it, *Adios,*
little house, you've been a good friend, though not
the palace we imagined when they first told us 'Venice' ...
It legal to drive, she asks, *when you can't stop crying?*

And so begins their long migration east, their route
as jagged as a cardiogram of a heart enduring stress,
the beat very nearly going dead when, in a little town
in Texas, they get that drunk they fight and in the tent

that night when Amy farts, Sabrina whispers to herself,
It's worse than fucking Zyklon B ..., prompting Amy to crawl
on all fours out the flap, stagger like the victim of a random attack
to where, very nearly asleep at the wheel, you might have

picked her out of the night with your lights, swerved and left her
in your rearview mirror, backlit by dawn's pink mushroom
cloud, watching you vanish like she'd just seen the flash
of her life passing through her so that later, in New York,

she would sit down to type, having rolled up her sleeves,
though not before finding in her desk's bottom drawer
the page of notes on which you'd scrawled, *The Chair*
in American History. And underlined it not once but twice.

Levittown

Psychoanalysis? No. Never. No need. But in the '50s, my partner, yes.
For many years. Later we discovered he'd been one of Hoover's boys. I
laughed! She used to say, 'But he does me good!'

SABRINA WOLF, AUTHOR'S INTERVIEW (UNPUBLISHED), 1987

The ceiling, ordinarily brown, is coming on slowly like a short-order grill –
the sun as it sinks on New Jersey being deflected by the venetian blinds –
and Amy, supine on the couch underneath, feels her face begin to burn
while the man to whom she's entrusted her soul retains his right to silence,

dickering on his notepad, as Amy blubbers on and on about some doll
she calls Sabrina, rows and rows of Sheetrock homes over each of which
he has sketched a bomb and embossed it with a hammer and sickle,
    thinking,
The Chief? His dick? It big? It small? Hard to know, him a single man and
    all ...

Then, to indicate the rate at which each bomb is falling, he adds quick ticks
like strings have snapped and Amy broaches masturbation, the guilt she felt
when she was small, doing it on the bathroom floor, *Sometimes I did it ...
Twice a day!* Ah that's disgusting, he thinks, and gives a groan which Amy

understands as intensely sympathetic. *It's a guilt that's grown as I've got
    older ...*
Her face by now is awfully red. She fast approaching the point of
    combustion?
He wears his hand like a surgical mask. Any wonder the Chief has kept
    himself
to himself, when any man of fibre would. He sighs, You only have to think
    of Christ ...

Christ! And then you got these Jewish broads. They are the primary conduit
of Commie infiltration. He draws a house, scribbles it out and in frustration
    says,
*Okay, Miss Glinkelstein, I think that's enough for today. We'll meet again on ...
Tuesday? Can I suggest, this guilt of yours, might not its source lie somewhere
    else?*

She nods, dries her eyes, and as she leaves the pink blinds cool through purple to grey.

He reaches for the phone and dials his wife, who answers on the forty-ninth ring.

What she want the phonograph in the bedroom for? – *Hello?* ...

He lets her squirm ...

Hello? ... She a little out of breath? – *Hello?* ... Boom! he thinks and the line goes dead.

Company

You were walking down Main Street, USA, in 1953.
It was two or just after in the morning. You'd a copy of *Charm*
in your briefcase and you were musing like some guy out of Sophocles,
Ti kerdainei to zen. Though not necessarily in the original Greek.

You'd just killed an hour in an Atomic diner – stuck a knife in its back,
stirred it about like a spoon in a cupful of coffee – where the waitress
had been friendly, from Utah; in her forties and extremely good-looking.
About her you could only assume, *She musta been let down by her cookin',*

when pausing at the entrance to an alley, patting your pockets for
    a cigarette,
your green eye's caught like a cat's eye by the flare of a Zippo being
    flicked,
illuminating like faces etched out of the dark two faces like the faces
    of men –
Two men? Up an alley? Are they queer? – lean enough in the cheek to be

Communists? For you've spent the last year reading *Capital*, in the spare
    time
allowed you by the company, for which you have worked all your life,
though tonight your head hurts, having banged it, being a Jew, on the
    ceiling
of your office where each morning, before you arrive, your door's brass
    plaque

has been spat upon by the Negro, who regrets it at once and wipes it with
    the cloth
he is carrying, chuckling as he reads: *Middle Management – and yet, we
    regret,*
no higher. Still, there's a clock in it for you if you stick to the end.
    We import them
especially from Switzerland. It'll cuckoo to you for what's left of your life ... So,

Commies, queers, whatever they are, like dancers, cheek-to-cheek, doing
     the tango,
their fingertips tender to you their old Zippo, prompting you to think,
     Life, the bottom line? –
although this time perhaps in the original Greek. Without moving your
     feet you lean
into that alley, take a suck from the flame and lean out again, turn around

and walk back to the diner, where the waitress smiles when you offer
     her *Charm* –
Whaddaya thinka that Marx as an ethicist? – and seeing what looks like
     a light
in your eye, tells you about her cabin in Utah, the husband she buried,
     upside-down
in the dirt, the breadknife still in his hog-hairy back. *Wanna run?* you
     suggest,

run for our lives? Nothing nicer, after all, than a doll in deep doodoo, and
     she closes
her eyes, like you're a breeze from the south, and she's imagining lying on
     some
beach in Brazil – not a stitch on her! – as you blow apart the pages of her
     heart
like a book and she says, swinging off her stool, *I think he's cool. Lose the
     suit.*

The Fifties

There's a little Eames rocker, pink-shelled, in the corner
and in it sits a woman, almost naked. Fifty, fifty-five, maybe older,
striated by the moonlight in the blinds, she has covered her face
with both her hands, refusing to be a party to what's being done to her.

If it weren't for her hands she'd be looking straight up, at the fan
rotating on the ceiling which, in turn, turns the air on her nipples like dials,
concentrating so hard, with its fingers so light on the heart she has
so carefully encrypted. She's a deep one. It ain't easy. Will it crack her?

There's a Buick sedan in the street outside, parked in the shadow
of a palm tree, the trunk of which sprouts from the trunk of that auto.
Sitting in it are two men so dissimilar we could call one Chalk, call one
    Cheese.
Chalk is lean, Okie-faced like a farm-boy whose roots withered up in the

dustbowl (though later in life he'll be outed as the only extraterrestrial
to have slipped through the net that was Roswell, prompting his move to
Alaska, where he still runs a cheap chain of laundromats). Cheese, to
    his right,
is a fatso whose beetling brows breed beads of sweat, like lanterns being

jiggled in the middle of the night from the eaves of a shack in Las Cruces,
by the banging of his Paw taking out on his Maw the frustration at the mess
of his life, until – with the rocker rocking faster and faster – they drip
on the crotch of his pants which is as taut as the teepee of his boyhood.

Oh mercy, Sabrina, have mercy! sings the woman in that little Eames rocker.
I've a secret that they're trying to find out. They want me to spill it and you're
    helping ...
So great is the pressure she's under that you'd guess there's no way she'll resist
until Chalk, being Chalk, he passes wind – *Why pardon me, Blimp, for being*
    crude! –

And Cheese, he socks him so hard that the head blows, *PLUGHT!*, spraying
    luminous shit
all over the shop and, dangling inside out down the shirtfront, what had been
    the face
is in tatters. Neckhole continues – neckholes do – to cough up spluts of flobby
    goo
till from it crawls ... *What the hell?* ... something of a shock? It happens though.

Fact is, it happens a lot. Still, it's the smell of the fart, not the look of the goo,
that really repels our friend Cheese. Yet by the time he's wound down the door,
flapped it all through and Chalk has squeaked *Hey, what'd I do?* her big secret
    is out,
she's proved you right and they have just gone and clean missed it. What a pair
    of putzs.

Four Short Poems from the War on Communism

Tom and Bob

In the early hours of a Tuesday morning two men emerge from an alley –
of a type from which two cats might well have appeared the more likely –
then, pausing on the threshold of society, succumb to a certain uncertainty.
What's just transpired between them, is it something they should shake on?

Cognisant of the Buick, its lights out, beneath a pink sign that says G—MEN—,
one flips up the collar of his trenchcoat, one brings down his brim like a visor,
and then they go their separate ways like lovers who'll one day wake in Moscow
as two men might in an ICU and take a while to remember how they got there.

Engagement

Ten past ten that Tuesday night
wife of Tom, wife of Bob
dial each other's number
and find that the lines are engaged.

Elm Street

It's a phenomenon some people find it hard to explain –
how a Buick parked in the wind and rain to the right
of the elm outside Tom's house can, in good conscience,
lay claim to being the Buick, elm's left, front of Bob's place.

Not that it matters to the wives who wait, reflecting at length
as the dusk comes down – cigarette one hand, buck-me-up
the other and the boys having trooped off reluctantly
to bed – on what the hell those two guys are doing out there.

The Skeletons

It's about a year later that they wake up one morning
and find the Buick has been towed away overnight,
an oil stain on the street where it sat for so long,
and it's as if, of a sudden, life's that little bit brighter.

While the Buick is being dumped in a field full of Buicks –
each of which in due course will contain two male skeletons –
the Moms announce that it is time to get packing ...
Two households in mayhem, kids packed into Packards,

and though Tom's ex on Elm turns right and goes east
while Bob's ex turns likewise and goes west, the kids like crazy
from the rear windshields wave. *We'll write!* they mouth, a promise
to which they will all stay true, except for Bob's eldest, whom they
    excuse,

having flown home from Vietnam in a coffin and been met by
    The Medal of Honor.

Dead Soldier

I can honestly say that of all the missions in which I was involved
during my twenty-two years with the FBI, it was the summer I spent
in Wichita holed up in a cheap motel room keeping tabs on two dykes
whose house we'd filled so full of bugs it was as bad as an infestation

from which I took the greatest pleasure. Marilyn was up there, it hardly
needs saying, especially that night when the Big Man fucked her
and she put me to thinking about the whores in Japan, their pretty little
faces with their eyes screwed shut like squeezy dolls, getting wheezier

and wheezier. *What a blessing,* I'd thought then, *The Bomb has been* ...
But Marilyn? She sure got to know what the world weighed that night!
And yet she never came close to my pinko pair who were in terms of pure
soap opera on a par with *I Love Lucy* though it could have been the heat

of that Kansan summer contributed to the feeling of delirium I had, the way
my room began to stink, the manager acting a kind of suspicious, sniffing
like he thought it might be me was the problem. Shot down, he told me, over
North Korea, taken and tortured by the Chinese ... I looked out one time

at three in the morning and I saw him lying flat on the lawn like a corpse,
a highball still in his hand like a hard on. The heart goes out to a guy
    like that
but when I bent to take his glass, he sat up straight, there'd be a man
along in the morning, he told me, yes siree, no worries ... I remember
    distinctly

the last of his liquor spilling on the grass between my feet ... The weeks go by,
I fall in with their rhythm, listening to the things that go on in a house,
the radio, the television, the fridge door opening and closing in the kitchen,
Sabrina grinding the dark-roast beans without which her life would not have

been worth living, for to tell you the truth I quickly realised that The Wichita
    Two
could not have lit a fire in a matchstick factory. I just lay there, my mind
like the ribbon of their incessant typing, until one day I woke and all I could
    hear
was the wind getting up. I saw a leaf make the sign of the cross at my window.

It was, I suspected, a wake-up call. *They're gone*, I thought, *gone south for the winter*

So I collated the tapes, drove all night and when I got back to DC put in a call

to a girl had been sweet on me in high school. Divorced, kids, we met for lunch.

And it was one of those days you get in that city when you feel like a man

can do no wrong, now that the heat has gone out of everything. Her teeth were false

from a beating she'd taken. She'd gone to town on foundation. Her eyes had come

prepared to understand anything and although she's now dubbed me Daddy-O'Two,

I still like to lie on the concrete roof of our condominium, listening to the beltway.

Witch

Amy takes her seat and the junior senator from Wisconsin –
whose eyes have Amy's face feeling freshly bathed in acid –
waits for the room to assume a deathly hush, then asks,
Miss Glinkelstein, are you now or have you ever been ...?

Though Amy is convinced that she's not, she's a little unsure
how to answer. The kliegs are very bright, the room so much
smaller than it ought to be, given the testosterone packed into it.
The question hangs in the air like a hook so she takes off her coat,

avails herself of it. At this there's an audible in-taking of breath
and she finds in herself such a sense of exposure that when
a wiseguy in the press, from the corner of his mouth, suggests
sotto voce, *Spill 'em, baby, spill 'em!*, she smiles, in all innocence,

and unbuttons her bodice, and takes it from where her attorney
lends her his hand up onto the table and, apart from her hat –
atramentous, ill-chosen and that not to speak of her scarlet stilettos –
to the beat of the gavel like the clacking of castanets, copper-bot-

tomed naked she dances and is beamed through the glittering ether
of the greater metropolitan area, causing men to stop bug-eyed
upon passing store windows where, quite possibly, *never*
have so many men experienced ... in public ... together ... before the
    networks

blink, come to their senses – mindful that their duty is to print lots of
money – it falling to some schmo to pull the plug on not only
the camera but also the kliegs, leaving Amy, the air so full of smoke
from Camels, Kools, Winston Kings, no option but to climb down,

re-dress and in her still hot mic confide how out of breath she's got.

Soren Asleep

Soren is running as fast as he can from a gap in the dunes towards the sea.
He is wearing no clothes. He is clearly excited, not unlike an American
    prisoner of war
the love of whose life is a Vietnamese widow who has fallen to her knees,
    her arms
outspread, weeping sea-green tears of joy, backlit by the sun as it sets
    like jelly,

which is strange because the taste that he has in his mouth is the
    gun-metal grey
of a tongue's taste. *Tongue?* Stick to *Gun*, I promise it'll better prepare you
for the fact that while Soren is dreaming the door to his closet
    slides sideways
and a neat little lady in an hourglass suit extracts from her crocodile
    clutch

a weapon so big it's too big to be grasped by just one of those little
    white hands of hers.
She cocks it nonetheless with her chin, steps to the bed and takes aim,
    pausing only
to note, as well she might, how his eyelids are like a woman's on the
    cusp of climaxing.
It's a little revolting and, having turned away her face in clenched
    anticipation,

she applies to the trigger two fingers of pressure and so obliterates not
    only his head
but the pillow on which it was resting and leaves in the mattress such
    a big bloody hole
she could stick her hands in, right up to the wrists, and come out
    with two fistfuls
of wadding, which turn – upon closer inspection – into greenbacks
    squirrelled away

by the victim whose torso continues in its duvet to spasm while the
    down, duck-plucked,
in the moonlight floats with such an ease of motion that the moralist in
    me has no hesitation
in pointing out the salutary contrast it makes to the spume of all that
    blood and brain
spattering off of everything, cardboard boxes, ashtrays, the lamp with
    its jelly-red shade ...

It's an awful shame. That dream was such a good one. What's with the
    broad? She got issues?
The littleness of the hands? Their whiteness? The matter of an hourglass
    suit? Stop! Stop!
You're killing me. Let's put ourselves out of our misery. *Hey little lady!*
    Go give us a clue ...
She dips her lips to the barrel and blows. Soren opens his eyes. The closet
    door is closed.

The Lady from Avon

You might be a man – though not, it's true, the man you once were –
who thinks to himself, *Aren't Remingtons great ...* and so begins to type
the clickety clack of her heels on the street, secure in the knowledge
that your wife is downtown, working hard for the boss of Big Firm Inc.

Your house is located at the end of the street. When the doorbell rings
it gives you a jolt and you stop what you're typing, you need time
to think. You pick the cigarette from its saucer – the last of a set, it came
with the house, boxed in the basement, each item wrapped in old
     newspaper.

This dame at the door, she a redhead? Real tall? You take a deep drag
and are tempted to peek, to stretch out your neck like you might stretch
     a point –
lay your cheek to the glass and conjecture, *Is she in the pay of the FBI?
A honeytrap?* Or just the lady from Avon whose patina may struggle

but whose patter adapts to the abnormal fact that you're the man of
     the house –
not the house's housewife – and to whom it turns out she's at liberty –
if so broad a concept can be got through your doorway – to pass, on
     the q.t.,
tips on complexion, yours – and she frowns – the ever problematical
     hammertone.

In what you've come to think of as *The Saucer of Sorrows*, you screw out
what's left of your cigarette and, discounting unwisely your former
     conjecture,
succumb to the charm of cosmetics. *Men do*, she tells you, having
     hoicked up
her skirt, the better, she says, to straddle and get at you with
     itty-bitty bottles

of blusher and tubes, then stops right there, leans right back, looks
     down her
long, strong nose at you as if she's wondering what to make of a
     housebound hack
in whose homunculus-like hands – *They hairy backed?* Natch! – a lady's
breasts might meet their match, she to shake out her hair and coo,
     Honey? I'm home!

The Pornographer

One Luxo lamp is black, one Luxo lamp is white,
but they're equally keen to read what I'm about to write:
One lovely horse is white, one lovely horse is black.
Like lovers they stand for hours, scratching each other's back.

A Round of Golf

The brain only thinks what it thinks it thinks,
thinks Amy, preparing for her inaugural drive
down Fairway No. 1 of this old famous links,
but hips are where it's at in a stance as lithe

as hers is; that and the kind of follow through
at which Sabrina shouts *Hey, that's a whistler!*
then takes to the tee herself. Her drive is true,
she keeps it low, *Take that up the ass, Mr Hoover,*

you can almost hear her say, chucking her club
at the caddie who thinks (or thinks he thinks)
Willya look at her – tartan pants, a tartan cap,
a turtleneck by Pringle, all in clashing pastel pinks.

Still, he loves them both. He hefts their bags
and staggers briefly; double-bent he steadies up,
then off he goes like an early jet-propulsion crank,
accelerating to a jog, his eyes upon that rising bank

of cloud complete with not infrequent thunderbolts.
Uh-oh ..., he thinks (or thinks he thinks). The girls
are waiting by their balls; the second shot
is oh so vital; the wind around them howls and swirls.

He recommends, as always, caution – *Pitch it short,*
Percentage golf. They listen, nod, then ... go for broke.
He rolls his eyes. The clubhouse lights look like a port.
C'mon! shouts Sabie, *Giddy up! You ain't that kinda bloke.*

The Paperboy

Amy Glinkelstein's *The Chair in American History*
is published in the fall of '61 and meets with a silence
so profound that Amy hears the proverbial pin drop
and takes it as a sign that the last eight years have been

wasted. But then again she's philosophical. At least
that's that done, she thinks, and hefts it with both hands
up onto a shelf. The passing months become a year
and her nights increasingly disturbed by pages

being turned like the wind would turn them or a mind
whose conscience won't allow it to sleep, each page
a day being taken from her until suddenly Sabrina
is pressing down on her shoulder, the wind has knocked

the candle over and so dry is the book it catches light.
Amy! Amy! It's over, it's over ... She reaches out for her glass of water.
They were reading my book, she would say. *They were
going to find out what I wrote at the end of it.* She takes a sip

and can smell herself, cold, clammy ... herself again, dull
and extinguished. *You won't ever leave me, will you, Sabrina?*
Sabrina appears to ponder this and they lie until dawn lights
the leaves in the curtains and the silence is broken by the crash

from the porch of a pot of begonias being knocked over
by that Sunday morning's *New York Times*, which contains
the first considered piece ... *This book is nine hundred pages long.
Eight hundred and ninety-seven of those pages are about chairs*

*and the people who made them. They are well worth reading.
You'll learn a lot. The last three pages are also about a chair.
But a chair of a different sort. These pages seem to me
to be the greatest three pages of prose ever committed to print*

by an American ... And the telephone begins to ring. Off the hook.

The Creeps

Heart of Ruby by D.D. Wolfwhistler was the kind of book
which gets tossed into the lake of the American mind
and sinks straight to the bottom, where sediment quickly
covers it, and if it weren't for the creeps, the bottom feeders,

rooting around with their bad eyes in the murk made worse
by the muck they stir up as if they're being led by a sick sense
to what all feeds their creepy needs, there it would have stayed,
eaten by its own acidic content, taking revenge on the lake that way.

Instead, one creep read it and blabbed about it to another creep
who asked to borrow it and, when on receipt of a deposit
the loan was agreed, went home and spent the day devouring it.
And that night the second creep told a third creep to get the fuck

out and find its own copy and before you knew it every
damned creep in the lake had read it and tattoo parlours were
doing a trade in creeps who wanted that heart from off of its cover
to adorn some private part of their creepy anatomy or other ...

Next thing was you got this creep who was proud of being a creep,
possessing as it did the rudimentary makings of a backbone,
and so it wrote an effusive appraisal – *I laughed! I cried! I spoilt Luigi!* –
and sent it off to an editor who, though not himself a creep,

had sympathy for creeps and may even in his youth have repressed
the first stirrings. He read, rewrote, lopped off the final sentence
and as much to put paid to the sight of himself on the surface of stuff,
thought, *Goddamn, I'll publish!* Whereupon Sabrina at breakfast

nearly choked on her toast. *About time too!* she spluttered
then went and rooted out the sequel and had it FedExed to her agent,
and one can only smirk at the incredulity with which *Heart of Jet's*
ascent to number one on the *New York Times* bestseller list was met

and at the ease with which the funds were found for the penthouse
apartment – described by that same newspaper as *affording views
of Central Park to die for* and *a floor whole forests wouldn't cover* –
in which Amy and Sabrina were to live out their days, high and dry.

Apartment

Amy and Sabrina are Birkenau bound
when they find that the door in the floor
of their wagon is not, like so many doors,
closed to them. What have they to lose

when the locomotive balks at a fallen fir –
there will always be one, it is often a girl –
by letting themselves down, lying flat
on their backs, then holding their breaths

until such time as the girl has been dragged
by her hair to one side, stripped, raped, shot
and the wagons again begin to roll like a dream
from which they'll eventually wake, sit up

and look over their shoulders as the taillight
vanishes where the trees like wives close ranks
to protect it? *Let's go and see what they did to her,*
says Amy, getting up as if nature had called her.

They find her dumped in a ditch full of water,
become again the tree she began as, and they
scratch their initials in her bark and a heart
with a nail Sabie's jemmied from a sleeper.

They will learn to survive on nuts and berries.
The trains become more frequent, then stop.
The wives are won over when good wins over evil.
In the winter the forest proves hard to heat.

States of Anatomy

Minnesota

Amy comes home from work, opens her blouse and looks at her breasts
like a man might quickly look away from two sisters sitting shoulder
to shoulder, their backs to a dancehall wall so thin they can feel it
being peppered by snowflakes blowing over the border from Canada.

Texas

Amy sometimes thinks of herself as a cave a child balked at the mouth of,
so that when, at the age of forty-six, she gets taken in hand,
shown the way, it almost blows her head off and Sabrina, on all fours,
can only do what she can, like Jackie Kennedy that day down in Dallas.

New York

Taller than all but the tallest of men, Amy is not what Sabrina calls heavy
and so suffice here to say that at Woodstock she appeared to tower
above everybody like a reed waist deep in water
which rocks very slowly one way and then just as slowly the other.

California

Not since the late Neolithic has hair of all kinds enjoyed such a rage,
taking to the streets in defence of the lengths to which it is prepared
       to grow ...
Still, one has to ask: is there another pair of 'pits here as hairy as Amy's?
Were each hair a thread of saffron she'd be worth her weight in gold.

Florida

There's a part of Amy's anatomy would be of fascination to the best of us.
In the middle of her chest, a little to the left, it will sometimes beat
a little too rapidly though by no means as rapid as a hummingbird's
       heart ...
Poor little bird, burning sugar, one sweet-lipped flower very much
       like another.

North Carolina

Forgive me (don't if you don't want to) if I return to Amy's breasts,
which are more than made up for by her nipples. Sabrina, amused
by how long they can grow, takes them between the Vs of her fingers
like cigarettes. By the time she's smoked the one she's ready to light up
    the other.

A Poetry Reading

It is 1986, a poetry reading in Manhattan, and even if you're happy to allow
for it's being the heyday of post-modernism it's still a little hard to ignore
how the individual members of the audience – young, urbane, turtlenecked –
    are notable
entirely for their absence until in come Amy and Sabrina and take two seats
    at the back

beside a boy in a Bob's Stores T-shirt. *Hello Mr Middletown, Connecticut*, says
    Amy,
not standing on ceremony, *You at Wesleyan? You look like a poet. You a poet?*
Pretending to be deep in a book, *She mean me?* thinks the boy in the Bob's
    Stores T-shirt.
Oh! Spare me, please, groans Amy, *He's only sittin' readin' your damn novel,*
    Sabrina ...

When the boy looks up it is all he can do not to faint. Amy digs Sabrina
    with her elbow,
She'll probably sign it for you though I have to say she's gone and gotten awful
    aloof
since them Swedes took such a shine to 'er. By the way, you got to Chapter 10 yet?
That twist happens Chapter 10? That was me, I thought of that. I just like to put
    that out

whenever I get the opportunity. Keeps the record straight. For posterity. Sabrina!
You gonna say hello to our new poet friend or are you not? You mind us chattin'
    you up?
We're women of a certain age, you understand. We don't get taken much notice of
these days. In fact, to be honest, we barely even notice each other. Isn't that right,
    Sabrina?

Amy ...? says Sabrina, her black eyes ringed with wrinkles, smiling ...
    Shut up.
You've been a certain age since I met you. Amy raises her brow at the Bob's
    Stores boy
as if to say, *You hear that? Wha'diditellya* ... It is then that a young man steps
    to the lectern.
He taps the mic. *Thank you*, he says. *Thank you and ... goodnight.*
    Whereupon Amy claps ecstatically

and doesn't hang about for the shouting. Sabrina rolls her eyes and smiles
again and then
she reaches for the book on the Bob's Stores boy's lap and pauses – *May I?* –
before taking it.
Her fountain pen is gold with pink and turquoise inlays. *Be nice to see your
work*, she says.
*But isn't Amy a terrible natter! Still, she's always out on Wednesdays, some big
architectural committee ...*

When she hands back the book she has signed her name with such good
grace and exuberance
that the final 'a' of Sabrina fills the whole page like a heart and inside it is
written her phone number.

The Meals of the Day

Breakfast

Sabrina wakes up in a mood so black that even a cup
of black coffee can't lift it. When Amy refuses
to bring her another she lies there twisting her pubic hair
like the handlebar moustaches of a well-waxed general.

Morning Break

A cup of green tea in a glass? A slice of watermelon
when in season? Not for Amy the bars of black chocolate
whose foil she'll find between the sheets, irreducibly
wrinkled and golden like the faeces of some mythical beast.

Lunch

Sabrina skips lunch like a heart skips a beat
and it leaves her feeling weak in her heart a little later,
like the beat her heart skipped is a beat skipped for ever.
I should be beaten on the bottom with a stick, she thinks.

Afternoon Break

A porcelain pot of Darjeeling? A scone with jam and cream?
No. A pretzel, a Pepsi, taken on the hoof, or an apple
if she's on a health jag ... The traffic lights changing from red
to green. A park bench, certainly. But in fall or in spring?

Dinner

Sabrina is almost always late. Amy prepares it alone,
but rinsing a zucchini like a man masturbating only fills her
full of sadness, so much seed going to waste for the want of a cunt.
Where the hell is she? thinks Amy, chopping it up into chunks.

Supper

Having put new black sheets on the bed, Amy takes off
all her clothes and spreads herself into the corners
like marmalade. *Oh*, thinks Sabrina, annoyed,
It's going to take me hours to lick every inch of her off.

Soren Does What He Can to Help

It's the kind of joint, a little louche, where beneath a cloud of cigarette smoke
a black girl and a white girl can take a table and talk and be thought none
the less of by the guys at the bar, just glad to think the thoughts that make
of thinking such a pleasure and who can count amongst their number – tonight

a night in this respect a lot like any other – an example of their kind so tall
were you to lock him in a box, hoist the box upon a trailer, set out across
the Midwest, you would find there folks, no strangers to the big concepts of
1) being asked to stand in line and 2) being parted from such hard-earned dough

as you see fit to charge for a gawp inside your box at him in a suit a size or two
too small, collar, tie none too tight and – at a speed easily in excess of what has
hitherto passed in that town for life – his red hairline receding ... the kind of guy,
in other words, on whom a little walk-up on 10th exerts no real attraction, given
     how

at home there the cockroaches are like a big happy family extending ad nauseam,
and for whom television is so increasingly compelling – *It's such a hot appliance!* –
that after they had watched it loads, felt intensely moved by Frank Costello's
     hands,
they'd crept up its legs and got in it. *Mere matter of time before they 'ave their
     own soap,*

thinks the guy at the bar, gently nursing a Scotch when the joint, it jolts and
     then –
Jeez! – starts to rock around a lot like they have gone and got a super, dropped it
on this town to test – *They? Being who? Hard to say*, tipping back his drink he
     thinks
and in the dark like lightning strips ... Where once there sat an ad exec whose
     own

dark heart he hardly knew, despite the boom that from it came, now stands
     a man –
left hand holding up the roof – whose incandescent chest S brands the minds
     of those
he'll save that night, as when between two girls he kneels and to their brows –
     one
black, one white – his palms impart what we now know to be cold, hard science.

The Appliance

Washing Machine

In that Apex Electrical washing machine designed by Henry Dreyfuss
to resemble the kind of space vehicle that would one day take people
    to Venus,
Amy dreams, one stormy night, that she has landed on a queer little
    planet
and, opening the hatch, about to step out, is excited by the prospect
    of a clean start.

Drill

Sabrina buys a drill, a Skilsaw Model 250, and carries it from
    room to room –
Her brow the V of vigilance – taking aim at whatever needs fixing
because no man, if Sabrina can help it, shall darken the door of her house
or be more like a man than the shape of a man cut from his own
    undipped headlamps.

Television

Amy is content with the radio until the appearance of a '48 Admiral –
blocky like a Bakelite robot with a face that could be anybody's –
brings her to her senses. Later they'll discover, somewhat to their horror,
that it is possible to watch as an A-bomb explodes and not leave on the
    sofa your shadow.

Refrigerator

Sabrina opens the fridge – a Westinghouse and white, taller than
    herself by a foot –
then looks away like one would from the light in an execution chamber
and so sees, framed in her kitchen window, her neighbour at his own
    kitchen window,
smiling to himself at the figure she cuts, glancing guiltily over
    her shoulder.

Camera

Amy buys Sabrina a Kodak, a gift for her fortieth birthday, a day
    they spend fishing
on a lake in New Brunswick where, despite or because of the nip
    in the air ...
Twenty years later, a brown paper bag, back of a wardrobe with dry rot,
Amy comes again on that old reel of Kodachrome and thinks, *The hell!*
    Why not?

Lawnmower

Amy is mowing the lawn with the mower of tomorrow, a Bohn,
when her mind is struck like a stroke by the thought of tomorrow
    not coming ...
The grass will grow, run wild, pink flowers appear like mad ideas and
    their neighbours' eyes
in passing roll – spanning the unspoken, *A jungle!* – across the sky
    like rainbows.

Hobos

Had Amy and Sabrina been men –
two men? Why not two hobos,
their sad rags flying in the face
of fashion as they run to catch up

with a freight train which they've
reason to believe might be going a place
name of *Anywhere else but here! –*
they might have first met in a boxcar.

Two men in a boxcar, crossing America,
time on their hands like the dirt
that gets worked ... might they not
have reached out in the night for each other

and found a kind of warmth there waiting?
Their kisses lasting longer than the
prairies they're missing as the steel tracks
hummed and their hair turned grey ... O!

how I do hope so for I have often imagined
what it must have been like to have been a boy,
abed, in the middle of America, a farm boy perhaps
with his window wide open, for whom that

lonesome whistle blows and accompanies
his sense of a journey being taken – from where,
where to, he can only imagine – by way
of where it is that he finds himself and loathes.

What Thomasina Told Me
from Seven Thomasinas

It stood five miles from our town as the crow flies
or as I would have flown on my Spacelander bike,
a four-square concrete box of a building for which the word
that springs to mind would have been nonetheless a misnomer

and set in so vast an expanse of that grass which in Kentucky
thrives – the latter uncut since the building was built,
though that is to suppose that *built*
is the word and not something weirder like *appeared* or *arrived* –

that you could never quite see it until you got closer,
whereupon it would rise, without any windows, just the ladder
up one side which was rusted real bad by the time I first climbed it,
having plucked up the courage just to see what was there

though in no way expecting to find what I found, the absence
of a roof and way down on its floor, a lady on a towel,
her head in a book. She said, *I thought there'd be someone
come sooner or later. Are you just a head or do you get better?*

She rolled herself over in her towel so it wrapped her, sat up
and patted the concrete beside her and so I threw my leg over,
I climbed down the inside. She was, it's true, considerably older
and I was a boy at an impressionable age. *You live here?* I asked.

She replied, *I survive. This building, I built it, in a manner of speaking.
It's my home*, she said and I believed her ... *What's your name?*
– *Thomasina*, she replied. *What you readin', Thomasina?* – *Well*, she said,
Aren't we the boy brimful of questions ... You're a little bit young but I'll tellya.

Self-portrait at Defcon 2

On the day that I turned one, Strategic Air Command stepped up
to Defcon 2 and the chrome dome glittered so in the clouds
above my cot. *Well, what of it?* I hear you ask, *Or am I
misremembering? Did North Dakota blow in a great big puff*

of buffalo gut? You got a point there of course. Minot? Its missiles?
One day. In the meantime, who'd've been assed? I was probably
just as safe as any little baby ever can be, my cheeks flaming
only with eczema and my eyes becoming cognisant of there being

truth in Forster's dictum – that thing he said, about connecting –
as I grew up in a town, the littlest dot on our school wall map,
– a line like a vein running into it, a line like a vein running out of it –
where the girls all had this habit of saving hard from the age of eight

and then, after nine long years of brutal self-denial which left them thin
like not uncomplicated paper, taking off for LA or the likes
so that it was with a sense of something lost being glossed over
that you might've come upon them in magazines later, pouting like
     money

was the be-all and the end-all. I prefer to think of them now as girls
who at the age of sixteen would've held your hand, gazing at the stars,
and who spent a lot of time worrying whether their breaths smelt,
in which respects we shared stuff – stuff that's had me thinking since

I should've said Yes once, I should've got on that big bus with her,
whispered in her ear *I got you babe* ... and had her rolling her eyes,
like she was Oh-So-Mature, at me acting the goof
with my hand on her tummy, pretending little babies were to die for.

Wedding
or Look Away Now

if you're reading in bed, smile at your lover asleep beside you,
yawn and lay *Lung Soup* aside. That, or your dreams may be disturbed
by a thousand rounds and maybe more from a weapon which, forensics
    claim,
would have penetrated even Kevlar plating, an outline artist, on his tenth

stick of chalk, scratching his head at the bumpy old ceiling where
an eyeball dangles by its optical cord, appraising the bed from which
it has sprung, like a work so expressive of all life in the raw it could not now
resemble less two lovers caught in the act of loving. Instead – modern,
    merciless –

it will not spare the young detective who to this tenement building
on Avenue X, with its windows framing like so many mugshots
the Italian stallion, the Yid with a lid, the manic Hispanic and the Pole
who's no joke, has come tonight despite his date with the girl to whom

he had planned to propose – so hard a heart has his superior,
dried up by years of pointless paperwork. The mugshots croon –
it is that kind of night – like an a cappella rat pack strobed by the cop car's
ectoplasmic light, *Blue moon* ... they croon it slow ... *you saw me standing
    alone* ...

and the young detective blushes, voice breaking as he barks at a sergeant
who is only two weeks from retirement and whose reply is the bubble
that he blows from out of his twisted mouth's side, until the thing
he is thinking could be scrawled in it: *Get outta my ass, little nigga boy.*

Go clean a few johns with that tongue o' yers ... On each landing
as he climbs there are ladyboys, clinging in little clusters like graces,
and though the odd one is as bald as a duck's egg, lippy in a way that
    ain't nice,
for the most part, on tiptoe, they're behind him, like the train a bride drags

to the altar, where the boy of her dreams with one brow slightly raised
(though his heart leaps like lips to kiss her heart) is backed up by his gang,
all those mugshots in tux, whose windpipes will all rise and be swingin',
like the wind in the wood of a mind, taken up from behind by great
    weeping.

The Moms

It's a little wooden treehouse two hundred yards high in a redwood
and the degree to which it sways, on a night like this, is precipitous.
What, one must ask, has possessed them? Had the weathermen and
    women
not explicitly warned every boy in the state to stay home with his Mom?

Or did they think that their tree would be somehow exempt, the storm
bifurcating like a river round a rock, and if that was what they thought
did they think of that river as a river of light, leaking into their house
through the cracks in its planks? If so, what would that have been like?

It is a question I ask in all sincerity, for while a more duplicitous poet
might opt to obfuscate, deploy some flashy metaphor, that's not a game
that interests me, deploying only in my need to illuminate. I give you
an example: of the candles they've a stack of, just the one has stayed lit,

its flame like the head on a Balinese dancer as it flutters on its wick
from shoulder to shoulder, lending an ear first to one boy then the other,
eyebrows rising, sway by sway, at the thoughts these boys got sealed
    inside them ...
You get the picture? Or do I need to spell it out – the treehouse, the tree,

the storm and the candle, either side of which lie our two boys on their
    backs,
in sleeping bags zipped right up to their necks ... Still, the storm will pass
like all storms pass, and the morning will find them in not two bags
    but one.
The candle having danced for as long as it could? They did what they
    done.

The rest is history. I'd quickly run through it if it weren't so well known.
Suffice here to say that having put their clothes on, climbed down the
    tree,
amazed what the storm's done, they sit back-to-back on a devastated
    stump
and think of their Moms, being single Moms, in need of love, in need
    of luck.

BACK STORY

Back Story

Amy and Sabrina are driving – where from, where to, who knows?
for although I am sitting in the back seat and can see between
the backs of their heads the lights of the on-coming traffic
I'm like a hitchhiker picked up and forgotten about when it's found

that he has nothing to say. Neither feels the need to look over
her shoulder to check that I am still there. I don't appear to figure
in their rearview mirror. Perhaps I've shrunk, become so small
that a crumb of blueberry muffin is to me what the muffin was to them.

Perhaps it's in everyone's interest that the top two-thirds of my face
is obscured by the hood of my Wicca Uni hoodie, on the chest
of which two *Hell Hath* eyes would have put the fear of God in all
but the couple who'd seen their own likeness reflected and so pulled over.

If it weren't that reading makes me sick I could, of course, claim to be
reading a book, squeezed as I am between two stacks like minders,
one highbrow, one lowbrow ... Or, given how baggy my khaki culottes,
could I be jerking off, scratching my ass, winkling wee bogeys and
    eating them

while wondering if it might not be wicked to crash when a full moon
looms above the crest of the road, they lean their heads together to kiss
and my mind begins very slowly to spin, the trees, the stars, the road
all rolling into one and leaving me to crawl from the vehicle unharmed

and, in a stillness broken only by a still spinning wheel, be suddenly alone
except for the moose (which Amy had screamed too late to avoid)
still there where it stood, backlit by the moon, on the crest of the road,
and watching me slip, it is reasonable to assume, back into the wood.

In a Photograph

entitled *Ready for Bed*, hand in hand like man and wife
(the man, as is common, considerably older),
Amy is wearing her pinstripe pyjamas, short of her ankles,
short of her wrists, Sabrina her baby-doll nightie,

which, apart from the decorative bow at her bodice, is cut
from some stuff so transparent she could as easily
be stark staring nude, given how cold, how unforgiving
the light which draws such blank expressions, the bed behind them

no less stiff than a car that's been parked at the edge of a cliff
and flanked by matching Biedermeier tables (*hers bipolar
with pills and thrillers, on his the gold Rolex chronometer
for which he has only himself to blame when – as he still has it –*

*he chose to step out of his office for a time but left beneath
his rosewood desk the much-loved pair of Italian loafers
into which would squirm the silky feet of a man
his wife had already made bold with – unwisely perhaps,*

she's no spring chicken herself after all). Yet what compels
about this photograph is not so much the women in question,
their expressions, blank or otherwise, but on the wall, above their heads,
mounted like men mount stags' heads or whatever other animal

they have cared to go to the trouble of shooting through the heart –
rhinoceros heads, the heads of bison though never, understandably,
the heads of giraffe – the head of some guy the photographer felt
like doing the honour of preserving for reasons best known to himself.

Two States

What more can be said about Amy's chest that hasn't already been said?
That it looks a lot like the salt flats of Utah where so many speed records have
    been set,
first by Brits like Malcolm Campbell, whose *Blue Bird* flew – metaphorically
    speaking –
in the fall of 1935 at 301.129mph – measured over a distance of one mile –

but then by men like our own Art Arfons, who held the record three times,
and the five times holder Craig Breedlove; it finally falling to Gary Gabelich,
in the rocket they called *Blue Flame*, to smash the record one last time
before things moved to the Black Rock desert where, in 1997, Wing
    Commander

Andy Green – another Brit to boot – was the first to put his foot to the floor
and – upon letting it all hang out the back – punched such a hole in the old
    sound barrier
that his record still stands as I write. Extraordinary men, flatness a boon to
    them,
which is, to so many men, the equivalent of an eight-hour movie by Andy
    Warhol,

who got a little giddy when he first met Amy and she told him – with a
    straight face –
the story of how she'd been born in a barn, *The biggest barn in all Minnesota!*
And that night Andy lay in his bed, wishing and wishing and wishing and
    wishing
that he had been a little baby, born in a barn in Minnesota, the barn doors
    opening

as the rooster crowed, the sun rose up and a man with an axe came,
    cut the cord,
took him to the pump, washed him down, spun him in the air like a football
    for joy,
and that on that farm he had been reared, passed down a line of
    tow-haired daughters
until it was the turn of the last in line, who whispered about her not being his
    sister

at all, how his mother had died one snowy night in a Salvation Army
    Red Shield Hostel,
and when he started to cry, pleading with her to stop, had wriggled
    her nightshirt
up into her 'pits, taken his hand, which was limp, by the wrist and
    with its icy fingertips
stroked what would, one day, she feared, be as big a pair of breasts
    as her big sister

Beth's, until he'd fallen fast asleep and she went on stroking, stroking
    back and forth
like she might have had Asperger's – which would only later begin
    to be diagnosed –
while Andy's eyes, beneath their lids, followed each stroke like
    a Xerox machine,
making photostatic copies, going over and over and over and over
    the surface of things.

Double Act

For such an ostensibly humourless woman Amy's orgasms
come quick like jokes as if all along Sabrina had held the key
to her basement where thousands of cans with the labels peeled off
lay covered in cobwebs like the cobwebs were a cloth – nearby
a copy of *How to Survive the Bomb and Why* – can after can
after can after can, just waiting to be shown the sharp edge
of a tongue and the laughter let out at the press of a button.

*

Sabrina's orgasms were different, they had no political content,
going on and on like shaggy-dog stories, increasingly making
no sense and ending only when she pissed herself laughing,
precipitating a dash for the water closet, where she'd stay
for however long Amy took to replace the sheet – having done
all she could for the mattress – and then re-emerge
like Richard Nixon, guilty but not to blame.

Havana

I was tunnelling under the Great Wall of China
when who did I meet, tunnelling out,
but a lady I'd last seen in Havana, doing the salsa
at three in the morning when the building
we were dancing in collapsed – they do in Havana.

We were shy to begin with, a little bit frightened –
it was dark after all and we didn't have a candle.
She whispered, I sniffed, her breath smelt rooty.
When our noses accidentally touched I was afraid
she might think me a little bit snooty but then I discovered

I could tell she was blushing so I blushed too
like blushing was a symptom of some new kind of flu
that it would've been impolite of me not to have caught.
Like two suns cancelling out each other, we kissed
and had a little think, then we agreed to kiss again

until not only were we kissing despite our lips
being muddy, we were kissing because our lips
were muddy and when we felt a worm wriggling
in the mud of our mouths we didn't think to stop and wonder,
much less to spit it out, for in the apple of our eye

that worm was the loveliest worm in the world
and we could not have been more happy – my tunnel
was hers and hers was mine! – sucking back and forth
like a noodle or spaghetti. Still, perhaps I sucked
too hard or she did. Perhaps we'd stuff we'd left unsaid.

I had a little sleep – it's not unnatural – and when I woke again later
my lady was gone. The tunnel she'd dug went on before me.
Someday there'll be light at the end of it. To her family
I'll come as consolation, I hope, though of my own,
I can't be certain. I'd hate to be her, blinking up

at them all, holding their noses at her strong pong.
Still, we all pong one way or another in the end
and when they stoop to pull her out they will notice
what wonderful biceps she's got though her legs will be weak,
hairy like roots. Perhaps a wheelchair will be brought.

Two wheelchairs at windows, worlds apart when worlds
like hearts can be so weak, collapsing at three in the morning
And going, for the most part, unmourned, picked over
by birds for bits of our past, tugging out tufts of hair
from the rubble, our bodies warm with worms like kisses ...

Those are hers wriggling in me now, dancing in Havana.

Three Road Movies

Departure

I feel like I'm the only child who long ago lost interest, in his parents
and where they were taking him, a future they claimed
they could see, through the windshield kept clear by the wipers,
lashing left then right, like an argument to which there's no end in sight,

and who now prefers to kneel on the back seat of their Trabant P50
and stare through the blur of its volatile engine at the driver
(and her red-haired companion) of a slightly more powerful P60
a consistent, safe distance behind since we all left home that morning.

Damage

On the edge of a New Mexican mesa I was sitting, shoulder to shoulder,
with a woman I'd met in Las Cruces. We'd watched the sun set like a movie
and now that the desert below us was dark, what remained of the highway
off which we had turned was a red and white striped strip of light –

blood cells, white ones heading east, red on the trail of the sun ... I'd slipped
my arm around her waist. Our lives had been nothing to write home about.
Only God knew how we'd got there. When the force that drove
our dusty lips to touch proved irresistible, did He flinch? Did He look away?

Destination

The car was large, black, but as it travelled west across the dustbowl state,
the sun on its roof, sunny side up where should've been belongings
or a chicken coop – *Gas station left behind it for dead? Ahead lie
another gas station? Would that be their word against the word in the wires*

that they're racing? – I saw it slowly elongate as the post-war boom
in speed kicked in ... Shotgun on the spare chair like a sign pointing
Thataway! I have seen their black car stretch horizon to horizon,
though it's gotten so fast it takes all day to go past and on into the
    night-time.

Murder Mystery

Let it all boil down to an Airstream trailer
about a mile to your right on the Mojave desert,
through which you are driving in a Pontiac Firebird,
with binoculars like a crab on the red seat beside you.

Stop. Get out. Watch it float on a lake of illusory water
and hope the sun doesn't suddenly gleam off it,
cause your eyeballs to incinerate in their sockets,
the smoke to pour down your cheeks like black water.

Ask yourself instead, *Should I drive any closer?*
Should I pull up at its door and get out?
Give an authoritative rap and on receiving no answer
scrape with my nails an eyehole in its dust-encrusted window?

Conclude – I beg you – *Better not.* You've a lover in Venice,
California, whose deliquescence is like manna from heaven,
what more do you want? Compensation for the gas?
Fine. Put your bill in the post to my publisher.

To have seen it from a mile away is sufficient. The binoculars?
Lock 'em in the trunk, let 'em cook, turn around
and drive home, not so much at your leisure as at a speed
just a little in excess of the speed at which a Firebird would be

comfortable. And if, two days later, on the Pasadena Parkway,
the thought comes to you of how the head changes shape
only gradually, growing longer, longer, longer, longer,
do not conspire to neglect that thought. Remember Mojave.

An Earlier Night

I am like the kind of man who runs himself a bath
and then forgets to take it. A thousand times, *Alath!*
he cries (he has a lisp) when in the morning he discovers
the bath he ran the night before like the last in a long line of lovers.

Housewives of Nebraska

Acire's eyes are blue – so blue there's no blue in them – her hair
    blue-black like a Finn
and so it's no surprise we find her driving town to town in 1953
in the pay of Norsk Appliances, demonstrating their refrigerators
    to the housewives
of Nebraska, amongst whose blonde and homey bosoms she generates
    a frisson of frigidity.

It's like she's ice for bones ... – No flesh a man could cling to ... – Cling to?
    Maria Huk pretends
to puke then slaps her son around the head, *Soren! How many times*
    I have to tell you?
Don't stare with your mouth open! Soren cowers and feels a freak,
    aged fourteen and 6' 2"
with hair like flames being twister-whipped into a complicated trope –
    the hair, the flames,

the twister's spout – that takes off of some tall tower's top, of a type
    that Soren's seen before
depicted in those comic books to which he weekly turns for succour
    and from whose windows
women lean, clad only in their negligees, their arms outstretched
    with hands palm-up
as if their wrists are in handcuffs, their cleavages, being ample,
    squeezed in order to propel

from throats like bells being rung for real the deathless cri de coeur,
    Will someone get me outta here!
– *Their lives in peril?* asks Acire. *They beseeching me for help?* She keeps
    her cool. *Now ladies,*
she continues, *these men of ours have appetites.* She smiles and rolls
    her blueless eyes
(she's learnt her patter from the book), *and so we ladies must provide the*
    most capacious of capacities ...

The fridge beside her does look big, *Like a type of box*, Maria thinks,
  Miss Norsk herself here
mighta been delivered in – her skin that pale it's almost blue. It's like fried egg
  white left to cool.
Acire thinks, *The face on her ...* as she removes the fridge's shelves and
  lays them carefully to one side.
Now she scans from wife to wife. Behind each wife there stands a man,
  taller, broader – *Are they for real?* –

whose hands are weights upon each shoulder and so it's with a sigh
  she says, *If only I'd a great big man,*
brave enough to volunteer ... Her eyes of ice alight on Soren and from
  them stare his own infernal face and hair.
Maria Huk looks on aghast as her dumb son now makes his move
  towards the great refrigerator.
Acire winks at Mrs Huk, *Oh my*, she says, *he fits! And ladies, look, there's*
  even room for one more ... Me!

And in she slips, waves and pulls the door behind her. The housewives
  of Nebraska? They gather
round Maria Huk, who seems unsure of what to do until she pulls herself
  together, strides to the door
and yanks it open ... In the middle of a wood, down by the lake, from a
  clapboard shack, Acire bursts
completely naked, squealing, stopping, looking back as if to reassure
  herself that some big beast is after her.

Meet the Family

OK, you find yourself in the middle of a wood, so far so familiar,
the sun flavouring icicles in the blackening branches, first lemon,
then orange and hey, before you know it, your favourite, strawberry ...

But you are not that easily fooled and you'd have got the hell out
of there fast as you could if you hadn't seen a shack a little ways off,
the atom-patterned glow of its threadbare curtains coming into its own

as you watched from what was rapidly becoming so dark a god-for-
saken place that getting out had ceased to be a realistic option, not that
realistic options have ever been your forte but anyway, it's the shack

to which you're stumbling now, convinced that you'll be welcomed in
by whoever has made that shack a home – a man with a wife? Two tow-
haired children? Walls all lined with books from Amazon? Crockery

flickering in the glow from the stove? You're about to think, *Be nice if
it snowed* ... when the first snowflake from the dark sky falls like the first
real indication you've had that this wood ain't what you thought it was

and it wouldn't take much for that first frail flake to become what has
in common parlance been referred to by folks as a *brainstorm* were it not
that the shack now rushes towards you at a speed for which there is no need

and you burst in its door like you've put much more than your foot in it
but then just stand there, panting, letting in a night no wilder than a man
like yourself who has been out in it and lived to tell the tale to this here

four-square, four-eyed family looking up from what must have been grace.

Two Wine Glasses

Pressed to Amy's breasts, the fevered creation of some outré designer
whose ogloid eyeballs testify to a brain that from a tender age
has fed itself on brassy girls in whose distress he read a need
for brassieres from whose apexes lasers blast the eyes of all such

slimy monsters ... That or some pseudo breast-booster device
sold through the small ads of *Charm* to a rapidly expanding
market of women to whom America offers – if it offers anything –
the promise that a girl – Depression-born – need only part

with a small subscription to some quack with a shed in Idaho
whose wife knows nothing about what he gets up to but spends
her days on her own small-holding, doing back-breaking work
from dawn to dusk and then from what she thinks of fondly

as her garden plucks basketfuls of dandelions to make the wine,
a contributing factor in his mind (like mine) going so quickly
to seed and causing from his dirt floor such theories to sprout
that his wife never gets to see him no more as if the theories have

grown and taken him prisoner, biding their time in the shed
until spring when, tenaciously tendrilled like the weird often are,
they push out through the cracks in the painstaking planks
and instead of a shed there's no shed anymore but this bush of

magnificent blossoms, pink ones mainly but also deep red ones
which, taken on the tips of such fingers as would lift them like eyes
being lifted to heaven, are allowed to exude – homespun, heady –
an aroma, the olfactory equivalent of *It's morning in America* ...

Robot Revisiting

Had Amy and Sabrina been woken at two or two-thirty in the morning
in a cold-water flat barely big enough to contain the bed like a holding pen
in which so many Irish immigrants would've loved each other, given birth,
died and, dead, awaited burial that it can come as no surprise when from

its not untarnished finials four pairs of NYPD cuffs hang like the bed
    is itself
a beast though it's never seen anything quite like this which may yet shake
its old arthritic joints to bits ... by their door being smashed to smithereens
and so lifted their heads from off of their pillows, looked over their
    shoulders

and seen (through the deeply green fug that the moon makes when
    it shines
through their deeply green curtains) the wired up arms of a robot, flailing
to some monotonous drumbeat through the door's more easily splintered
    timbers
but sparking at its failure to make headway ... it would have been
    Sabrina who,

thinking not untypically fast, unlocked the cuffs above her head
    and – small
and stout like Joan of Arc, had Joan of Arc been small and stout and
    not so much
like Ingrid Bergman – leapt from the bed and, in the buff, clamped
    that robot's
wrists securely so that in the morning they would find, its batteries
    all but done

with twitching, the culprit of their broken sleep and think how there's
    no sorrier sight
than a run-down robot in handcuffs whose attack on two women has been
    foiled,
except that when the morning comes and the El that runs behind
    the house
jiggles the bed, the pair of them in it, the cuffs, the curtains revealed
    to be threadbare,
and they wake to the rancid smell of butter, sit up together and rub
    their eyes,

it's to find that the door has been repaired and that even the little
     rectangular mirror
is still there on its nail, its crack intact, reflecting on the wall above
     their heads
where the Sacred Heart would once have hung when Irish immigrants
     lived there.

Self-portrait as a Hollywood Auteur

People are always asking me
when *Amy and Sabrina: The Movie*
will be coming to a big screen where they are
and what I always tell them is

that the big screen where they are is a fleapit,
that the fleas are not even the worst of it,
that the stains on the carpet are disgusting
and that they needn't hold their breath to be bathed

in the light of any movie of mine ...
No, what I always tell them is that things are in the pipeline ...
Yet people are, by nature, impatient,
they long to mark dates in their diaries,

so I like to let on that the casting's going well.
Tilda? they ask, *Oh how wonderful.*
And what about ... I glance at my watch like I'm bored,
then I lay my cheek gently to their cheek,

The pre-nuptials are being sealed as we speak ...
When I linger like a secret takes time to sink in, then just as gently
pull back with a wink, some squeal with delight,
some faint. It's the ones that faint that catch my eye

and as they swoon I pinch their drink, tip it back
and break their fall ... Later, in bed, smoking, flat on my back,
I'll watch on the ceiling as my blue pool plays host
to the shadowy shape of whoever she was, fallen ... or was she pushed?

End of an Affair

Who could be accused of wanting to be seen,
standing at their window with the curtains drawn back,
like a portrait of themselves, cut off at the knees,
behind a lace blind like an antique chemise

by the kind of man who catches the last train each night
and will often have a carriage entirely to himself
in which to fall asleep and wake up in a world
where there could be a war on and he wouldn't be concerned?

An Honourable Occupation

Had Amy and Sabrina been whores –
two whores? Why not, it's a living –
I might have met them once in Berlin
and felt big-hearted, felt like giving,

given how the cold had been doing
to those people what a man wouldn't do
to his own worst enemy, assuming
that our man weren't one of them Japanese.

We're talking skin, we're talking bone,
we're talking organs with the lights down dim,
their peepers so deeply sunk in their skulls
I couldn't help feeling I was being taken in.

There were children, of course, not to blame,
you'd find them crouching in corners like stoves,
the old, awaiting denazification, holding out
to their hot little faces their hands like explanations.

But by Amy and Sabrina I mighta been moved,
supplied them with all that their hearts desired,
bacon rashers, pantyhose and even got to feeling
quite the man of their house, walking around

tapping walls for bomb damage, thought of them
in the end as not whores in the slightest,
just two women who'd done what they'd done
to survive and to whom, on that last day

in Departures at Tempelhof, shoulder to shoulder,
both in their finest, I'da tipped my hat. *Ladies*,
I'da said, then done that thing that made them laugh
like I was quick on the draw and shot from the hip.

Wedding Bed

I dreamt I'd been given a bed for the night
in that part of Berlin which will always be Wedding
by one of those women, common in Berlin,
whose good looks have been toughened by being opened to doubt

and whose legs are so badly in need of a shaving
that you could, all too easily, succumb to the chore,
get down on your knees with a razor, a basin
and perform for that woman, while the men downstairs roar

and a song, of sorts, breaks out in Russian,
what no man has performed for her before,
and that despite the years that she has spent on this earth –
walking on it, digging in it, pissing on it, shitting in it –

and from which she might feel she hasn't had her deserts.
I don't know how the Russians could've known we were doing it
but the stamping of their boots didn't just shake the house,
it took the rhythm of her breathing to unheard of new heights

and I kind of had the feeling – young man that I was –
that what was going on was going over my head.
So I kept my head down until the stamping subsided
and I could hear the Russians spilling out into the streets, laughing

and bawling their heads off like children before dying slowly
into the night. I say night but as I took the razor to the sink to rinse it
the sky was already a little bit pink yet I felt pretty sure
that I hadn't slept badly in that bed I'd been lent in Wedding
    for the night.

Lung Soup

Amy and Sabrina have been running – from what need not detain us –
down streets where signs that life exists consist largely of garbage;
where windows wax a listless yellow and chimneys flying flags of sulphur
are cast in sharp relief by clouds which, low with snow, reflect

the cauldron at this city's centre. In other words the kind of quarter
where cats and rats hang out together; dogs are sometimes seen to stagger,
finding breath here hard to come by, then stagger on as best they can
or, failing that, in the rising heat of their own piss pools, stand

and perceptibly vibrate as Amy and Sabrina pass, hand in hand, though,
given how the street is cobbled, lucky to be wearing flats for, had
    they not,
that thing which as this poem began we felt so sure should not detain
    us would, by now,
would, by now, have caught and chopped them into pieces for the rats –

if not the cats – to feed on. So there you have it, the scene is set
(one part Kafka, one part Brecht, like I could just as easily have lifted it)
at which they'll not so much as glance, and on a *Mietskaserne* wall at
    which they'll not so much as glance,
I just have time to paint these words: *You've a big decision coming up.*

Should they turn left? Should they turn right? Had their hands not been
so tightly clasped it might have torn their hearts apart. There's a door
    ahead
and they opt for that. When the steps of the stairs are not always there,
they stumble, but then at the top there's a door to what looks like a
    cupboard

and once inside, shoulder to shoulder, their panting subsides to the
    point where
a little brass lighter ignites a clearly frightened face. It's the waiter!
    They gulp.
Having looked at the floor, having looked at each other Sabrina,
    thinking fast
pipes up, *We forgot to pay for our bowls of soup. We'd like to make it up.*

The Finials

Who wouldn't be a fly on the wall
of a bedroom barely big enough
to contain a bed whose brassy finials
could be so easily set ablaze

by the sun's once daily chance to shine
through panes of bottle-bottom glass
as it goes down between two stout
distillery chimneys, that scorch spots

slowly are appearing upon so low
an attic ceiling where years of poorly
maintained slating have left concentric
rings of damp to grow such moulds

as overlap, reflecting in their way the bed
whose mattress smells of saturations,
dating back decades already, sweat, piss –
let's face it – semen, sput out of cocks

too many to mention by men who've
bunked here overnight while on the run
from crimes for which – their hearts have
told them – a trapdoor will, one day, be opened

but where – unable or unwilling to peel away
our compound eyes – now lies a sight,
which like a book just fallen open reveals
its two most much-loved pages – is it Baudelaire's

Les Lesbiennes? – beneath four flaming finials.

The Organ Grinder

What happens happens without musical accompaniment
unless you're prepared to let in through the window
not just the organ grinder but the organ grinder's monkey,
the latter attired like a Professor Degener of Berlin University

to whose work on ethnomusicology the organ grinder stands
like a perfectly mechanical exemplum in lectures he has taken
out into the streets for the benefit of the people of Wedding,
from the windows of whose *Mietskasernen* red flags hang in the sun

like the washing which the workaholic women of Wedding
like to try to have done by lunchtime, though given the grinding
routine of existence, a sense of how pointless life can be
when boiled down to it, a heart can give up, a mind be snuffed out

and so provide the spark for another of Red Wedding's famous riots,
so many fists flying in the heat of the night that the monkey
thinking only of himself, abandons the grinder to the grinder's fate,
high-tails it up a drainpipe and takes refuge on the roof from where

(feeling braver) he'll scoop himself handfuls of mud from the gutter
and fling it at the cops, coming running with their truncheons,
until he gets bored, looks over his shoulder and finds a little window,
left a little ajar, through which he'll poke his tufty head and find it

in a bedroom barely big enough to contain the bed on which he'll see –
Or do mine eyes deceive me? – the bodies of two women lying flat
on their backs ... *Both naked,* he'll note with a frown so profoundly
wrapped up in its thoughts that the heavy breathing creeping

up behind him like a shadow fails to forewarn him of what's about
to befall him and the organ grinder grabs him by the scruff of his collar,
You little rat! he shouts, waking the women who see what they see,
assume that they're dreaming, make spoons and go straight back to sleep.

Exodus

Leaving behind them the kitchen like a kitchen by Schütte-Lihotzky
Amy and Sabrina have taken their drinks and gone and sat down
in the living room where a candle is doing what it's good at
which is to keep the darkness at arm's length like a Jew who just happens

have comedic gifts doing his best to keep everyone's spirit up.
Ay yi yi, he sighs, his eyes peeping over the collar, *My wick was not so long,
it's not getting any the longer.* Which is too bad; the light's doing wonders
for Amy's complexion, though Amy – and this needs saying – could
        not appear

harder on the eye had she been hewn from the cross Christ died on
by the kind of contemporary carver in whom a love of Late German
        Gothic
might be something he'd want to re-think in the future, if it's a future
he wants in the carving game. Yet Sabrina could not be more mellow,

her brown eyes proof if proof were required that not all German blondes
need be blue-eyed. She thinks, *She is beneath that blouse possessed
of the kind of small, no-nonsense breasts mine eyes would dearly love to see
come out fighting like a flyweight's fists in the hope that I might parry them.*

I think we can guess where we're going here. The bedroom door is a
        little ajar –
as bedroom doors so often are – and the candle sheds sufficient light
        to see
in there the promised land, a simple mattress on the floor, a chair with
a hairbrush, bristles up, like it might not be a brush at all but a part of
        the chair,

(to be thought on like some kind of experiment) when, like a man
        reaching out
to his own front door gets set upon by thugs who, even as they beat him,
remain indistinguishable from the shadows in which they'd been hiding,
the candle succumbs to a welter of blows. *Fight back, little flame!*
        Fight back!

I cry. But it doesn't ... *Are you frightened?* Sabrina's voice could not be
   deeper.
I certainly am, thinks Amy, whistling what can only be Schoenberg
until Sabrina stands up, *Will you come with me, please?* Leaving Amy
to wonder if God did the right thing, bringing grief to the people of
   Egypt like that.

Feuerland

How hard would it be to guess the weight of this door –
clad in iron, blackened (and blackened not just on the outside only)
by the smoke from the coal being burnt night and day
in the factories like trees bearing down on these streets –

as it closes now at Amy's back and sends a shudder rising
through as dark and steep a stairwell as Amy's ever seen,
at the top of which is a skylight, too dirty to let any light in,
supposing Berlin ever got any, which Amy is beginning to doubt,

when from where the shudder's gone to roost there comes a shout,
Don't hang about or the rats will get you. They have dirty little minds
and will run up your legs. Amy begins to climb what amounts to a very
    old ladder
and on every landing every door exudes a sense of disorder

until, at the top, she almost trips on a cast iron bucket of water.
To the door ahead, left a little ajar – backlit by the blaze
of a stoked stove chasing up the walls shadows like trees on fire –
a black cat has come to look out and miaow, *Well, will ya look at*
    what we got here ...

Amy looks up at the skylight, which she could easily reach out and
    touch now,
cracked like a pair of sig runes, as a bomber, bound for Tempelhof,
trickles its taillight across it like blood and the building, beneath her,
groans. Amy looks down at the cat which has manacled itself to
    her ankle.

She thinks, *Were I to knock now and the door to swing open,*
will Sabrina be waiting like Edward G. Robinson,
smoking a cigar, in a leather armchair, if it weren't for being so nearly naked,
there'd be no one she could look like less than Edward G. Robinson?

Hackney Central Ghost Train

While the East End of London in 2003 is not the West End of Berlin
in October '29, the driving rain remains the same on a metropolitan street
like the street that's lit up in my mind and now yours with shops past
which Sabrina walks, thinking, *How often one finds, next door to each other,*

*the fish shop and the flower shop standing shoulder to shoulder. It's as if
they've decided, what with freshness being all, that, having come from the sea,
having come from the soil, we're in this together, though our margins
may be small ...* on her way to the Palast to meet Amy where the movie

is the new *Frau im Mond.* Yet a pavement this wet is like walking on glass,
stained by the shops that Sabrina walks past, her brolly like a rocket,
blue in the rain, and her underneath it like a rocket's red flame
    which would,
I confess, sound a little priapic and for which I'd apologise if it weren't

for Sabrina being the kind of girl who's been happy to strap, in the past,
    when asked
by Gill – to give but one example – who would have gone and got
    all breathy,
snipping at her sightlines with her fingers like scissors, *Oh good
    gracious me,
Sabrina!* Which brings us nicely to the S-bahn stop where she runs
    up the stairs

just in case a train's coming, only to discover at the platform's end
    a man in fedora,
trenchcoat, spats. *Shit ...* thinks Sabrina, looking down at her watch,
    *that man
to throw himself down on the track, it's only going to leave me terribly late ...
Please Mister Weirdo, don't do it this time. You know what they say
    about acting*

*in haste ... Take a little time ... Think it over. There'll always be another
along in ten minutes ...* She takes out her compact, *There could at least
    have been a moon ...
What'll she think? A big mistake or will her heart and mine be like
    pulsars tonight?*
Which would have been an interesting thought to have had back then
    in 1929 ...

as the train screams in and Sabrina finds a seat in its electrified interior, wipes

like she's waving an eyehole in the glass and leaves me standing in the driving rain

yet, nonetheless, wishing her well, only sorry she'd to share in my interminable wait,

thinking, *You're never alone with a ... Oh come on will ya ... Light, for Chrissake! Light!*

Freikorperkultur

Amy and Sabrina have not yet met but they're sitting about five
    yards apart
on a plain wooden bench, polished almost black by the many
    bare bottoms
it has borne and to which it has imparted such lessons in discomfort as
accompany the lectures of Adolf Koch on hygiene, socialism, flakier stuff

while the light that falls and tries to warm the lumpen backs in rows
    like ranks
is in actual fact as chilly as the lecture is difficult to follow. *Still,*
    thinks Amy,
whose mind has begun to wander, having stolen more glances than
    she should
have done at Sabrina five yards to her right, *A better man? Be hard
    to uncover ...*

When the lecture ends and the benches have all been pushed back
    to the walls,
a space is created for gymnastics, around which the women form a
    circle to stretch.
They have such strength locked up in their bodies, yet told to touch
    their toes,
only Sabrina succeeds, placing her hands palm-down on the boards
    like a quadruped

with its head back-to-front and at odds with its neighbours who
    regard it, askance
in their struggle, bent as much by the passing of the years as by the
    efforts they
are making to let loose that strength to which the bosses of big business
    have thrown
away the only keys. *They think it obscene, I to kiss my own ass?*
    thinks Sabrina,

pushing off from the boards like a pianist whose hands are still wet
    from the depths
of Sonata 27 by Beethoven when suddenly someone passes wind, so
    loud and fast
that the tight asshole from whence it came can have gone unguarded
    for no more
than the instant of its breach by gases pent within its bowels and –
    because she knows

that she should not – Sabrina breaks into the fit of giggles which
    activates the pro-
lapse in her back. *Wind, Miss de Wolfe*, says Koch, *is a perfectly healthy
    phenomenon.*
*Mrs Glinkelstein, I applaud you on your freedom of expression, but can
    I trust you*
*perhaps to take under your wing this unfortunate creature and deliver
    her to where*

help will be provided entirely free of charge ... Amy's body by now
    has done the work
of a stove and lent to everybody her embarrassment like clothes in the
    rosy glow
of which Koch claps his hands, *Resume!* despite the clouds crowding
    like thugs
to the windows with lightning pinned to their lapels and rocking
    their big heads off.

A History of Pain

Sabrina's mother was not the prettiest
of a bunch of five Herero women
taken by soldiers in the middle of the night
to their munitions storehouse and raped

then driven out into the desert and dumped
where the sun spread their shadows
on the ground like a hand
on which it was counting *Eenee, meenee, mainee, mo* ...

so that only Sabrina's own mother survived,
confessing it all to a missionary,
the solitary white sheep of a family
whose money had come from coal in the Rhineland.

He fell in love. He touched her belly –
she assumed it was a blessing and thanked him –
and when, a little later, she died giving birth
he felt responsible. He took the baby

and that's how Sabrina came to be living
in a beautiful house near Dresden,
the implausible daughter of a much-loved pastor
who dies when she is five of cancer

and leaves her the house out of which she is tricked
by the black sheep who likes nothing better
than to lay himself gently in the palm
of her hand and beg her – yes, beg her – for closure.

And Pain's Alternative

Had Sabrina been born in the Ruhr
in November 1923, her mother
having proved incapable
of mounting even passive resistance

to the young colonial soldier
whose grasp of what he was doing there
had been as shaky as the glass
in his hand when he asked her in German

so broken that had he been holding out to her
a flower he'd picked up on the road –
down which he had marched to her pit town –
mashed by the wheels of an armoured car,

it could not have sounded any the sweeter
nor left her feeling any the whiter,
noting how he'd failed to rub off on her sheets
like the local men whose wives despised her

and who smirked when her belly began to inflate
and out came the fighter to be, punching the air,
kicking and screaming and not a thing a mother
would have swapped for all the money in Germany ...

she would have remembered none of it, least of all
the letter which instructed her mother to get out
and explains why Sabrina grows up, a shade
darker than everyone else, in one of Berlin's poorer districts.

Water Colours

Not before time the communist candidate for president steps down
and, like a storm cloud staggering on its legs of lightning, Hindenburg
takes his leave of the field for the last time. Wedding takes comfort
in that at least, and the KPD – ironically – goes from strength to strength.

Two years later Goebbels' murder puts a smile on everyone's face and,
although photographs of him dead in the gutter stamped in red, Attacked?
are plastered to walls all over the city, a young Romany in possession
of the dead man's wallet is picked up by police, charged and acquitted.

Franz Kafka's novel *The Love Affair* is published in 1933 and the author
is well enough to attend the small gathering arranged by his publisher
at which his editor, Sabrina, makes an affectionate speech, *Dora, my dear,*
cover your ears for I must tell what a tease this rascal is, such horrors

he tells me locked up in his drawer ... Amy, years later, will take him on a tour
of the new Bauhaus building in Berlin, designed by Mies van der Rohe.
A treasure of a day, says Dora, averting her red, wind-quivered eyes
from the trees which fling into his grave their once green leaves like hankies,

and they all drive back to the apartment in which Amy and Sabrina now live
and where, in 1953, the pact will be concluded which leads to President
Arendt and her famous speech on power to the first of the three great
communist governments on which so much of our enduring prosperity rests.

And me? I studied hard and by 1981 had been appointed head of
    our leading
psychiatric community where my innovative techniques have brought
the world to our gates, begging to be told how we work such miracles. Why,
only this morning in the garden I was saying to one of our oldest patients,

who came to us forty-odd years ago, barely able to tie his own shoelaces,
but who now likes nothing better than to sit by the river and work
    on another
of his delightful water colours, which our pastor tells me run out of his shop
like hot cakes, *Ah dear friend, if only they knew what work we've had to do.*

Lebensraum

The German girl's joy would not be confined,
like a Sturmführer screaming, *Lebensraum! Lebensraum! Lebensraum!*
and to whom our bedsit's skin-thin walls were like the towns
of Western Poland, affording no protection to the unprepared
    and vulnerable.

Like fledgling intellectuals our beds became our bunkers
and yet however hard we tried to dream our dreams of England,
no match were we for her – *The Hun* in all her glory! –
when with each fresh onslaught our bits stood up, being manly, aflutter

like flowers in a forest where at that time of night it's quite creepy.
What use had we for each other? Our vows just proved as porous
as had done Peter Bonetti. Oh! If only we had been there in 1966 ...
Instead, that Günter Netzer bestrode our sacred turf with his hair,
    shoulder-

length and so golden we could, in truth, no longer cling to the dream
that Bobby Moore's had been lovelier, and in the canteen, on the
    morning after,
Donald Greer – *by himself* – had about him that look all candles have
when the light of intellectual inquiry has given rise to a thin wisp
    of smoke.

Oh! seeing him there, toying with his sausage, so enfeebled of brain
that a bean he'd sucked clean of its tomato sauce was a thing
newly vested with wonder, I swore I would take the fight to Berlin
and so, ten years later, having landed at Tegel, I took a room in a flat
    with two gay blokes

who reciprocated with an interest in my well-being, their address books
    spilling
on the kitchen table until I'd drunk so much wine I had to ask,
    Am I whoozy
or have you spoilt me for choice? This one! Receptionist for a practice of
    architects!
And so it was that on Monday morning who would I bump into
    but Hilde.

Her buildings were winning prizes from Iceland to Tierra del Fuego,
    powered
by the wind and by the sun, by waves, and even dung. With cups of coffee
I favoured her and lingered, loving her handsome hand, its sense of flow
across each sheet of white (like linen) paper, until, one day, *Was that*
    a wink?

Here she comes now, letting herself in as ever without so much
    as knocking,
her big bike slung across her back like a horse that she has rescued
    from exhaustion,
having urged it on with thighs as great as Netzer's were that night
    when he bestrode us,
then standing there panting at the living room door and daring me
    to tear all her clothes off.

The Eleventh Hour

Any bad painting of the sun is worth its weight in gold,
thinks Van der Jagt, sent to investigate a murder
he did not commit but for which he will serve a minimum
of nine hundred and ninety-nine years in a maximum security prison

when the chair – an abominable outcome – is denied a judge who's known
to the local court reporters as *Fliederfrisch* by an extremely welcome
point of law which the poor man's attorney, asleep at the time,
dreams up at the eleventh hour when – as luck doesn't always have it –

he is roused by the judge's gavel, bringing order to the scene of uproar
which follows the ruling – *Inadmissable!* – of not just that piece
of last gasp evidence without which no trial would be complete
but a busload of Jehovah's (eye) Witnesses and the personal appearance

of the murderer himself, still spattered in the blood of his victim
and waving what the prosecution concedes is the hitherto
unfound murder weapon which I refuse – yes refuse! – to describe here
for fear of the damage it might do to the gentler readers amongst you.

Suffice to say it's the kind of tool with which you might feel more at ease
were you to clasp your eyes upon it and catch it falling from on high,
accompanied by those hairy hands which you have always found attached
to a man you first met way, way back in a Pentecostal tent near
      Baton Rouge ...

By the time Van der Jagt gets out the world will have changed considerably.
There'll be very few people about. It'll have got a lot hotter then colder.
Yet Van der Jagt's a man who'd be nothing – *Nothing! I tell you, nothing!* –
if it weren't for any bad painting of the sun being worth its weight in gold.

A Crooked House

To a city on the make a young man comes
and takes a room at the top of a house
where no one wall stands straighter
than the wall to which it stands next.

There's a window let into one wall –
one foot by one foot at head height –
and until the winter starts in earnest
the sun greasepaints it every night

like a painting influenced by Die Brücke,
its execrable orange, its black-backed
tenement proving style can't be faked,
unlike content. The artist, at least, had the grace

not to sign it, realising, perhaps, that his talents
lay elsewhere, in film, for example,
which jiggers along at a speed the equal
of the trains which pass that now monochrome window

and to which the cracks in the walls respond
by spreading out, linking up, growing
progressively ever more complex
while the young man sits, night after night, in a chair

as straight as the room is crooked, his face
in a book like he's trying to conceal it,
though from whom or from what it's impossible to say.
The book – let's peek – is *How to Build Yourself a Desk.*

O the hours he'll put in at that desk when he's built it!
Though he's already vowed to work only by candle,
its flame illuminating his head like a star –
A Portrait of the Poet in His Darkest Hour ...

Unfortunate then when he gets no warning –
apart from a momentary sense of inertia
when first the floor and then the chair
leave him sitting in thin air – the ceiling cracks him on the head

and the house returns from whence it came
which is to say, pretty much, such dust
as finds its way into the eyes of people
and results in a great deal of redness and rubbing.

Kitchen

It's a little traditional kitchen like a kitchen in your typical *Mietskaserne*.
It contains a stove, a sink, a rudimentary table; a green blind has been
pulled down the window as if to chart the decline of a poem that will end
in a darkness so total that even the whistling kettle will have lost the will
    to whistle.

There is always a fly in a kitchen in summer and this kitchen is no
    exception.
The fly steers clear of the kettle but there's a pot of blackberry jam
    on the table
and it likes to alight on its rim. In the pot is a bone-handle knife,
    like a ladder
down which the fly crawls. There are worse things a fly could be
    crawling down.

Take, for instance, this poem, the words crawling down it like eyes
    to their doom
but taking in details of the room as they go: black stockings bloating
    in the sink
where they soak, a loaf of black bread on the table, the brassiere
    dripping black water
from the line to which it is pegged into two simple white cups and
    their saucers.

Awful to think of that brassiere, the weight of the flesh it was made
    for, the wire it requires
for security. Those breasts, one wonders, where are they? Are they
    (are we?) at liberty?
Could two strong hands ... even as I speak? One thinks of blue-veined,
    marble columns.
One thinks of them buckling at the elbow. One thinks of one's face in
    the rubble.

Would you like to leave now? You can if you want to. The door has
     been left a little ajar.
One imagines, beyond it, a hallway, a main door with not one but
     two deadlocks,
the stairwell a haunt of light-hearted men and children who rush down
     it like water.
You can hear them in the courtyard like a fountain, watched, one assumes,
     by their mothers.

No? Too late. Like a black fly embalmed in black amber the sun must
     now suck itself under
while the kettle which began so manfully has already boiled down
     like I said it would.
Our legs may no longer be holding us. Let's sit here, just the two of us,
     and wait.
When the kettle turns red it will find us like the shades of those who
     sat here before us.

This Poem

There will, in this poem, be a window,
its dimensions a break with tradition,
down which a blind has been drawn,
a green blind with a red spot burning in it.

Who pulled down that blind and why
are both questions you're entitled to ask,
unprepared as you are to waste time
on a poem of which – with good reason –

you're already a little suspicious, let down
as you've been by so many poems which,
having come on strong to begin with,
get so boring in the middle it's as much as

you can do to drag your mind from line to
line like a rough beast slouching towards
its sister's house in Stoke until the only
thing you want to do is to close your eyes

and fall asleep ... Yet that's where this poem –
mark my words – will do its best to prove
its worth with a bed and proper cotton sheets,
a black quilt, a red star burning at its centre,

and me in attendance to help you undress,
pull apart the bow at the nape of your neck,
sweep you off your bare feet and carry you
to where this poem will come gently to rest.

Painting

Were this poem not a poem
but a painting of Amy and Sabrina
sitting a little apart, a window
at head height between them,

one's eyes might easily come to rest
on neither Amy nor Sabrina –
however kindly on those eyes
Amy and Sabrina lie – but on the window

in between them which holds
like it's holding at arm's length
a reflection black-lit by the woods
whose back woods hold so small a cabin

that on a table set for two
a candle only serves to show
the egg placed plainly on each plate
for what each plainly placed egg is –

one egg white, one egg black –
the candle catching in its glow
what will, when all is said and done,
be thought the shake that shook the shack

so that on one's eyes might finally flash
the double yolk those eggs give rise to.
Unfortunately this poem's a poem
and not to be so easily seen through.

Lung Soup: The Movie

A Synopsis

Amy and Sabrina are lovers. They meet in Berlin and are killed,
their deaths foretold in frame after frame by the lights of Berlin
on the blade of a knife made to spin on a marble-topped counter –
the marble top becoming clouds, the knife a Lancaster's propeller.

We first meet Soren on a derelict stoop, watching what's attracted,
as it were, to the light, like a two-gallon can of vermilion nail paint
has been tipped out the door of a boarded-up store, rain doing its best
to wash it all away – it would take it all night – when the door behind him

opens with a creak and we needn't even have him look over his shoulder
to know that it's Acire whose presence in *Lung Soup: The Movie*
is not to be confused with her absence from *Lung Soup: The Book*
apart, that is, from 'Housewives of Nebraska' which is sort of like a trailer.

There will be scenes of an adult nature throughout. Two men in a bed?
What's funny about that? Both men deep in identical copies of Musil's
The Man Without Qualities when all of a sudden their door bursts open
and some guy in a wig demands to know just who the hell they think he is.

Another? I'll quote: *Thomasina makes love like a gold digger should
and you have to admire her commitment to wealth when she ends pressing
down with both hands on your heart and from where your soul floats,
preparing to depart, you can see that she's done everything a girl could ...*

Van der Jagt is nothing if not his creator – a small man, paunchy, nothing
to look at – in whose eyes the sea's illimitable glitter (on which, far out,
two tankers pass) reflects a dreamy nature. And yet he falls – for fall
he must – short of finding out what's going on here. O too cruel creator!

Together as ever on a sumptuous sofa, two great big cans of Campbell's
    soup
appearing to float behind their heads while men at their feet entertain them
like devils, offering them, skewered on the tips of their wit, the juiciest
morsels of gossip in town, Amy and Sabrina can't conceal that they're
    bored ...

New York shakes, great trees erupt. When next we look a whitetail deer and a black muskrat have stopped to watch in the moonlight a mare being prepared by her stallion. While the deer appears to be transfixed the muskrat's eyes roll over its shoulder. *You're sick!* it says to camera

and from those of us watching in Smell-O-Vision elicits a squeak of
    You stinker!

The Babies in Summer

With each new poem that he composes –
turning over a leaf or a change of bed linen –
he will go to the town, to the telegraph office:
There's lead in the pencil yet, he says
through brass bars gleaming in the sunlight
And accompany it with the usual, please.
– The usual being, Sir? – Ten dead roses.

At the store he stocks up on a few provisions
then heads out of town taking leave of his seat
as the buckboard bucks at a poorly laid plank
and the sun goes down on the road right ahead
like an eye growing drowsier and drowsier until –
the desert having flooded with jelly-red water –
the road has come to nothing and taken him with it.

The End

Imagine sitting in a cinema, enjoying for the hundredth time
Eisenstein's *Battleship Potemkin*, when the couple in front begin to kiss,
their Afros blending gently into one voluminous nimbus,
blotting out that pram as it hirples down those broad Odessa steps ...

You'll have wondered already why they plonked themselves there
when the cinema is otherwise empty. Yet having found that you
cannot explain it your frustration is surprisingly mild: *But what can I do?*
Move to my left? Move to my right? I'm comfy enough here where I am, thanks ...

Seeing as how, in your mind's eye, the woman's scream has continued
    regardless.
It is as if with each new viewing your careful brain has been perfecting
the recording that it keeps for itself. You could pause it now, rewind it
    to the bits
that you like best, the meat, the maggots, the soup bowls swinging in
    the galley untouched ...

Full steam ahead! you cry instead, and the couple in front go on kissing
with a passion so distracting that only the parting of the imperial fleet
can catch their eyes like the waves dividing and reveal the life,
sky-high with hope that will soon have you fissilling in your pockets
    for hankies

as people more commonly do at the end of old Hollywood weepies (although –
and this perhaps ironic – I don't include in that the movies of Douglas Sirk,
a more substantial artist than he's been given credit for, despite being tormented
by producer Ross Hunter, who would implore, *Doug! Doug! Make 'em weep!*

Make 'em weep! I wanna see five hundred handkerchiefs! Still, I digress, we all do
    ...)
before the screen has gone blank and the lights have come up and the lovers
    have been
washed away by your tears and you've an usherette waiting like a slim silhouette
to check from the end of your row that you're not about to leave any litter
    behind you.

Ende

Amy lifts the lid which we first heard tinkling in 'The Beginning',
a poem I hold in great affection, for despite all its faults –
Le' me list 'em! – it was the first I wrote with Amy in
so that each time I've recalled it since, it's been as if what was bubbling

in that big pot was me ... *Looks like we're almost done*, she shouts
and whatever it is that Sabrina replies,
it puts such a smile on Amy's face that even when
she brings down the lid again I can still see her glowing with happiness.